# ROCKET MAN

## BY BRETT LANGLEY

This book is memoir. It reflects the author's present recollections of experiences over time. Some names and characteristics have been changed, some events have been compressed, and some dialogue has been recreated.

PALMETTO
PUBLISHING
Charleston, SC
www.PalmettoPublishing.com

Hardcover ISBN: 979-8-8229-5032-0
Paperback ISBN: 979-8-8229-5033-7

# CONTENTS

# INTRODUCTION

· · · · · · · · · · · · · · · · · ·

This story is a reflection of my life during the years while my dad was alive. It begins on February 28th, 2008, when I first heard the news about what had unfolded the previous night at his house in Riverview, Michigan. He and his closest friend Jack, who lived with him at the time, were brutally murdered during a home invasion robbery, and the house was set ablaze to cover the criminal's tracks. My dad's house was targeted as he ran a successful vending company later in his life, servicing the greater Detroit area. It was known that he kept large amounts of cash and cigarettes at the house. It was nine months after the crime when the DNA results came back from the house and completely changed the course of the investigation. The details of what actually happened and everyone involved are still a partially unsolved murder mystery.

After the crime, I was taking regular trips back to my hometown to pick up the pieces and bring my father's estate to a close. My background story unfolds as a collection of memories during flights back to Detroit, reflections on old photographs and memories triggered through current events in my life at the time. My reflections on the past have been a way for me to handle the grieving process by reliving some of my most cherished memories and the moments when I was able to spend time with my dad. My story captures a complete cycle of life with me coming into the world when my dad was thirty-one years old and then my son being born when I was thirty-one years old.

The story ends with a dream that I had after returning home from the trial. In my dream, I put myself in my dad's house the night of the crime, knowing vaguely what had happened based on the evidence presented during the trial. Being in his house that night, I was able to course correct the events that left a permanent hole in my family. Through my reflections on the past, I realize how precious life is and how it should never be taken for granted. Anyone's life can change at any given moment by losing a loved one or when that time comes for you leave your loved ones behind. I hope my story is a reminder to appreciate those who are dear to us and enjoy every moment we have with them. This story is dedicated to my dad, whom I love and miss very much.

# THE AFTERMATH

.....................

It was a typical sunny afternoon in Newport Beach, California, on February 28th, 2008. I was working out of my home office and my wife Jennifer had taken our seven month old son, Jake, to a doctor's appointment. My cell phone rang, and seeing it was my mom, I thought it was unusual for her to call me mid-day during the week. I answered, and she asked me if I was in a good place because she needed to talk to me about something serious related to Dad. My parents had been separated since I was very young and weren't in regular communication with each other so I knew something was terribly wrong. My mind raced at what the news could be, and I asked what was going on. She told me there was a fire at Dad's house, Jack, who lived with him, was found shot dead in his bed, and my dad was missing. I struggled to process what she was telling me, and my immediate thought was that Dad had been taken hostage somewhere as part of all this. My dad ran a vending machine business in the greater Detroit area which was a pretty shady industry. She told me this all had just happened the night before, so the police were still trying to determine all the details as to what happened and who was involved. My mom lived in Atlanta, GA but had heard the news through one of her friends who lived back in Detroit. She told me how much she loved me and would be available anytime if I needed to talk while we worked through all of this. When we got off the phone, I immediately called the Riverview police department where Dad lived. I introduced myself as Dennis Langley's son and wanted to talk with whoever was in charge of the investigation to find out the latest. They took down my info and said they would have the lead detective call me back as soon as he was available. After I got off the phone, I scoured the Internet, trying to find any news on the incident, but it was all still too new. I paced around in the living room downstairs waiting for Jennifer to come home to tell her what was going on. We had plans to cook dinner at the house that evening to celebrate our four-year anniversary. Jenn pulled into the garage and walked through the door with Jake to find me completely distraught. She could tell by the look on my face that something really serious had happened. I began to explain what I knew so far and was waiting to talk with the Riverview police department to get the latest.

Later that afternoon, the local news in Detroit covered the story in front of Dad's house. The reporter said police were investigating a homicide and a missing person case, which took place the previous night at the house behind them in an upscale neighborhood in Riverview, Michigan. The news footage showed yellow police tape across Dad's driveway, the doors & windows were boarded up and the roof of his garage was completely gone from the fire.

It felt like days later when I finally received a call from the lead detective at the local police department. He introduced himself, filling me in on everything they knew so far, but I could tell he wasn't telling me everything as he was very vague. The detective told me that Jack had been stabbed, shot, and found dead in his upstairs bedroom. He said they believe Jack was home alone in the house when he was killed. The detective said they believed the intruders were there for the safe located in the garage, and Jack had returned earlier than expected from he & Dad's Wednesday night bowling league. He said the criminals had taken the safe in the garage and started a fire at the house with the intention to burn it down to cover their tracks, but the fire department was able to put it out before it burned the main portion of the house. He said it looked like the criminals started the fire in the garage and placed accelerants throughout the house to spread the fire. He said they found Dad's work van on fire parked on a side street a few blocks from the house, and were unsure of Dad's location. The detective said they had leads and were actively questioning suspects but couldn't provide any further detail at that time. The detective gave me his direct number and said I could call him any time, but he would keep me updated with their progress.

That night, I couldn't sleep. I spent the whole night in shock, staring at the clock until it was a reasonable time the next morning to call the detective to get the latest details. When I spoke to the detective in the morning, he said they had found another body in the garage at the house but had yet to confirm the identity. I knew immediately it had to be Dad and could hardly process the whole situation. The detective said they had taken three teenagers into custody. They believed the main suspect to be a girl named Alison who was the daughter of Dad's ex-girlfriend Rachel. They were also holding Alison's boyfriend along with another friend of theirs. The detective mentioned that the police had previous reports of Alison breaking into Dad's house, but he had never pressed charges. The detective seemed confident that they had those involved in the crime but told me that he couldn't discuss all of the details of the case as it would need to come out as part of the trial, which would take some time.

It was the next morning when the detective was able to confirm that the body found in the garage had been identified and was my dad. His body had been burned so badly from the fire that they had to identify him through dental records. I needed to get back to Detroit and started to look into funeral arrangements. Jennifer's parents dropped everything, and booked a flight right away from Denver to Orange County to watch Jake while we made plans to head to Detroit. Through my family's recommendations, it was decided to have Dad & Jack's funeral at the Trenton Chapel with the Martenson Family of Funeral Homes. The funeral was scheduled within a week after the night of Dad & Jack's passing. Considering the condition of Dad's remains, it was decided that he would be cremated.

Leading up to the funeral, further details of the investigation started to surface. Dad's cause of death was from multiple stab wounds. It was determined from the autopsy that there wasn't any smoke found in his lungs, which means he had passed away before the fire was started in the garage. It was determined that Jack had been stabbed and shot many times while asleep in his bed. While in custody, Alison had provided a confession to the crime, and the three teenagers remained in jail without bail. The detectives told me it would still be a few weeks for them to complete the investigation at the house before they could officially turn it over to me.

It was hard for me to sleep even though I was exhausted. Whenever I would start to fall asleep, I would wake up abruptly after seeing these short, violent, and gruesome clips imagining what had taken place in Dad's house that night. I kept seeing this quick moment of the expression I imagined on Dad's face when he came through the side door next to the garage and was surprised by the intruders. I had to constantly stop myself from wondering about the condition of his body when he was found in the garage. I was eager to take possession of dad's remains and have him with me moving forward.

The next morning, we needed to catch our flight to Detroit. We lived in a small neighborhood called Canoe Pond in Eastside Costa Mesa which was only a few miles from the Orange County airport. We all piled into Jenn's SUV so her parents could drop us off. Jenn's parents had made plans to stay at our house with Jake while Jenn & I traveled to Detroit for the funeral. As we pulled up to the front of the airport, we got out to say our goodbyes to Jake in his car seat. We made our way through ticketing, security, and to our departure gate for Detroit. We boarded the plane and got situated in our seats. As the plane took off, we looked out over our beautiful beach town, and the plane disappeared up into the clouds. Sitting next to Jennifer, I laid my head back on the seat, closed my eyes and my mind took me back to when everything all started.

# MOTOR CITY ROOTS

....................

When I was younger, my dad told me a story about a time before I was born when he and Mom got mugged at gun point in downtown Detroit one evening as they headed to an Elton John concert. He never told me the details, but the story always stuck in my mind, not because it was a great story but because of how I imagine Mom & Dad looked that evening and the imagery of the whole situation as if it were a scene from a cool movie.

I see them in the early '70s silver Corvette that my dad had bought for Mom. Dad is driving wearing his black fur coat, gold rope chain necklace, and the chunky gold link bracelet he always wore. He's got longer dark hair and his usual mustache he had my whole life. Mom is wearing big lightly tinted gold sunglasses, and her bleach-blond hair looks gorgeous laying on her fox fur coat. As they drive through the snow and slush-covered streets of downtown Detroit, the rumble of the V8 overpowers the '70s music playing through the car stereo. They approach Olympia Stadium with the sign reading "Elton John," and there is a long line of cars waiting to park at the venue. Too impatient to wait in line, they drive off to the neighborhood side streets to find parking. After finding a spot a few blocks away, they park the car, do a little bit of cocaine together, and then leave the car, walking toward the stadium. They are in a rough part of town, and considering the way they are dressed, they look completely out of place. About a block from the car, a group of guys appear out of nowhere and approach them. One of the guys walks up to Dad, pointing a gun at his forehead as Mom breaks down in tears, scared of the whole situation. Dad is frozen with a stern expression on his face. He's locked eye to eye with the gunman as the man instructs them to hand over their fur coats, jewelry, and money. Dad hesitates for a second and then tells my mom to give them what they are asking for. They begin taking off their coats and jewelry. Dad hands everything over along with a huge wad of cash folded over and kept together with a rubber band. Once the guys have what they were after, the gunman lowers his gun, and they run off. Dad watches them run down the street as Mom hugs him tightly in relief. Dad comforts Mom briefly before heading back to the car to get off the cold city streets of Detroit.

It was 1973 when my parents first met in downriver Detroit. My dad came from a large hard-working blue-collar family. He grew up with five brothers and two sisters. The entire family was raised in a one thousand square-foot house in Wyandotte, Michigan, which is a suburb about thirty minutes outside of Detroit. My dad stood out in the family with his trendy fashion style and always chasing after new business ideas with his entrepreneurial spirit, looking to make a buck. He was the quarterback of his high school football team, but he was better known as a fast ice speed skater. Dad was a good-looking guy who always had a pretty girl by his side.

When my parents met, my mom was eighteen and working at a clothing store in the local mall. My mom grew up in Livonia, Michigan, which is a few towns over from Wyandotte. She came from a smaller family and only had a younger brother. At the time, my dad was twenty-nine and owned a couple of trendy '70s clothing stores called the Bottom Drawer, which sold bell-bottoms, butterfly collared shirts, rock T-shirts, posters, and smoking paraphernalia. Dad earned the nickname "Rocket Man" among his close friends as he drove a van painted like the American flag with a rocket mounted on top and the name of his clothing store The Bottom Drawer painted on the side. He also owned a popular bar called Moby Dick's that showcased local bands while he worked behind the bar at night. Dad's biggest source of income was a growing business selling marijuana around the greater Detroit area. My parents were originally set up on a blind date through a girl who worked for my dad at the Bottom Drawer. She thought my dad would like her young, petite, blond friend named Becky. When my parents met, it was love at first sight, and they were always together from that point on.

Mom started managing the Bottom Drawer stores during the day while Dad made his way around town selling marijuana to a growing customer base. They would meet at Moby Dick's in the evening with Mom running the door and Dad serving drinks behind the bar. The bar was always packed with a young crowd coming to mingle and check out the local bands. From time to time, Mom got jealous checking the IDs of the girls who were there to see my dad behind the bar.

During a trip to Toronto in 1974 to buy clothes for The Bottom Drawer, Dad proposed to Mom, and they got married later that year. The newlyweds bought their first house on Twenty-First Street in Wyandotte. It was a small two-bedroom brick house with an upstairs apartment that my dad rented out. On April 16th, 1976, I was born into the world. My dad was thirty one and my mom was nineteen at the time. Shortly after, my dad sold Moby Dick's and opened a third clothing store called DJ Toronto. My mom no longer managed the clothing stores and was now a stay-at-home mom. Dad managed the stores while continuing to expand his marijuana business. The cash started to roll in, which allowed them to afford sexy cars, jewelry, and trendy clothes. My parents always dressed me in the trendiest and coolest clothes. They grew my bleach-blond hair out into a longer Beatle style haircut, which I decided to change when I came across an old pair of scissors in our garage and cut my bangs off the day before we were to take a professional family photo.

For the first three years of my life, we lived in that small house on Twenty-First street along with our big black Bouvier dog named Token, who got the name after eating a bag of Dad's marijuana. We would take Token out for walks with him pulling my dad on roller skates, and I would try to keep up on my little electric three-wheeler. I remember getting excited in our house when I would hear the intro song to *The Dukes of Hazzard* come on the TV and loved the sound of that orange car driving around in the country. A few years before I was to start kindergarten, my mom wanted us to move into a nicer neighborhood with better schools.

In 1979, we moved into a nicer two-story house with a large unfinished basement on Brandywine St. in the upscale Riverview Forest neighborhood.

My elementary school would be a short walking distance, just a few blocks from the house. For my third birthday, we had a large party at the new house. During this time, VHS cameras had just come out. Dad had one of the first VHS cameras available along with a Canon 35mm still camera and loved capturing my life growing up. He was always dressing me up to make sure I looked cool for his videos and photos. He filmed my entire third birthday party, interviewing all of our family and friends during the celebration before bringing out my new bike, which was a candy apple-red Schwinn Stingray with a yellow banana seat.

As I grew into my bike and could ride without the training wheels, BMX bikes came out as a growing trend. I told Dad how I thought BMX bikes were cool and asked if we could make my Schwinn look like a BMX bike. Shortly after, Dad took me to a local bike shop called Petri's in Wyandotte. When I walked into the shop, there was a strong smell of rubber from all of the BMX tires on the wall, which is still one of my favorite smells because I associate it with the excitement I felt that day. Dad talked to the guy behind the counter, asking about converting my Schwinn Stingray into a BMX bike, and the guy explained the biggest differences were the seat and handlebars. When we got back to the house, Dad grabbed some tools from the garage, and we hung out in the driveway while he installed the new components. Once he was done, it looked like an entirely new bike that resembled a BMX bike. Dad grabbed the video camera, and we headed over to my new school to capture some videos of me riding around at the large playground.

As the money continued to roll in, Dad bought a white two-door Cadillac Eldorado with red leather interior and chrome spoked wheels. He made a video of us roller-skating in front of the house while my grandparents came over to test drive the new Cadillac around the neighborhood. During this period, I had become obsessed with Joan Jett's "I Love Rock N Roll." Dad bought it for me on vinyl as my first record so I could play it on my toy turntable in my bedroom. I used to love opening my upstairs bedroom window, placing the record player on the ledge, start the record on full blast, run downstairs to the garage, grab my bike, and ride around out front, listening to the song until the end. Then it was time to run back upstairs and repeat the process.

Dad bought a second house on Walled Lake. It was a small house that he bought because of the lake front property. He tore down the original house and built a large modern cottage. The house had an indoor Jacuzzi and large theater room. We had a white-and-metallic-blue jet boat along with a paddleboat docked out back. It was a party house for friends and family to enjoy year-round. During the summers, we spent many days out on the boat, racing around the small lake in the jet boat. Beers and cocktails were always flowing at the house with '70s rock on the stereo.

During the winters, Uncle Chuck would plow snow off the ice to create a hockey rink. One winter while plowing snow off the frozen lake, his big lifted Chevy truck broke the ice. As soon as he heard the sound of cracking ice, he opened the driver side door and jumped out onto the stable ice next to the truck. The front end of the truck crashed through the ice into about eight feet of water just off the shoreline of the cottage. It was a sight to see with the bed of the truck sticking up out of the frozen lake and the whole front end under water. I watched from the sliding glass doors in the living room as my dad, Uncle Chuck, and friends stood on the ice in their winter clothes, working on pulling the truck from the broken ice with the help of a local tow truck. During those winter months, the snowmobiles also came out of storage so people could race around the frozen lake and venture through the nearby woods.

Around this time, Dad had sold off the clothing stores and opened up a liquor store called Langley's Liquor and Lottery, which generated the most lottery sales in all of Michigan. He had also started up a new business venture based on an invention he came up with called TeeWizz, which was a little automatic teeing device for golfers. The device was to be sold to golfers for practice at home or at the driving range to eliminate the constant need to tee up golf balls. Dad leased a building in Wyandotte to start manufacturing and assembly of the devices. To market TeeWizz, Dad hired a production crew to create a TV commercial with the golf pro Andy North. My mom and I got to be in the commercial. There were little clips of us using a TeeWizz, hitting golf balls that led up to Andy North teeing off a perfect drive far off into the distance saying, "Right down the middle."

Dad had multiple revenue streams, but it was the growing marijuana business that he ran out of the basement of our Riverview house that was generating large amounts of cash. He had hollowed out the stairs going down to the basement as storage for marijuana. His primary source was a connection down in Miami, Florida. He had a few guys who were runners that would drive down to Florida and back with cars that had the rear seats hollowed out. The marijuana would be stored in the rear seat through the trunk, and then rear of the back seat would zip shut so that nothing would be detected by anyone looking into the car.

Dad bought a small house in Fort Lauderdale for the trips down to Florida, and it was also used as a family vacation home. One of my favorite memories from the Fort Lauderdale house was from 1981 when a new TV channel was set to air for the first time—MTV. Dad was excited about the new channel, telling me they would be playing music videos made for popular songs on the radio. The day of MTV's launch, we had the TV on all day in anticipation as the channel displayed a countdown leading up to the very first music video to be aired. We were so excited and gathered in the living room, counting down the final seconds as if it was a New Year's celebration. Once the countdown was over, the channel showed footage of the Apollo 11 rocket launch, then it transitioned to an astronaut planting a flag with the MTV logo on the moon right before the very first music video was played. It was "Video Killed the Radio Star" by the Buggles. The launch of MTV was so exciting, and everyone was glued to the TV, watching history unfold. There were only a handful of videos at the time, and they played continuously.

As it was nearing time for me to start kindergarten, Mom was concerned about Dad dealing out of the basement. She expressed her concerns about the neighbors potentially catching on and it having a negative impact on me in school. Mom told him that he needed to transition out of the business within the next year before I started kindergarten. Because he was addicted to the lifestyle and the amount of cash it was generating, it was hard for Dad to wind down operations. He didn't see any harm in marijuana and felt that it would be legal someday. He wanted to capitalize on it while he had the opportunity as it also helped to fund his other investments in real estate, Langley's Liquor and Lottery, and TeeWizz. I was so young at the time that I had no idea what Dad did for work or where the money was coming from. Looking back on it all I think Dad was ahead of the times as marijuana seems to be on a path to full legalization and has become a big industry all these years later.

The time had come for me to start kindergarten. I can remember my first day of school. I walked over to the school wearing jeans and a navy plaid shirt carrying a red vinyl briefcase with my supplies that had zoo animals on the front. Dad drove slowly alongside of me, videoing the whole journey with '80s music playing from the car stereo. I liked being in Dad's videos but style was everything to him so I always had to look perfect. I can remember him telling me in the video to turn my briefcase around so that the graphics printed on the outside were facing the camera. I remember feeling cool strutting to school and looking forward to my first day.

During that year, the school hosted an annual fundraiser event in which students could sell various soap products from a catalogue. My mom took charge, having me call family members and all of Dad's connections. I would ask for potential support of my school fundraiser, offering the various soap products I had available for sale. Everyone was so supportive, and in no time, we had completely filled up the order sheet provided for the fundraiser. As Dad's customers stopped by the house to buy marijuana out of the basement, they would also place generous orders for soap on the way out. When the fundraiser came to an end, I had largely outsold the whole school, which was kindergarten through fifth grade. Based on the soap orders from Dad's customers, it was obvious he wasn't winding down the business. The principal was in shock at the amount of sales a kindergarten kid had generated and wanted to meet me in person. Leading up to my scheduled meeting with the principal, we had taken a trip down the Fort Lauderdale house. I picked a bunch of oranges off our tree in the backyard so I could bring some as a gift. I walked into the principal's office with a box of oranges, and he thanked me for being such a big part of the success of that year's fundraiser.

One of my friends lived about five or six houses down the street, and his mother was a teacher at our school. We met in kindergarten and would take turns playing at each other's houses. Suddenly he stopped coming over, and when I would go to his house, nobody would answer the door. When I saw him at school, I invited him over, but he told me he wasn't allowed to play with me anymore. When I got home, I told my mom what had happened that day. She decided to call my friend's mom down the street. When my friend's mom answered the phone, Mom asked if everything was ok, mentioning the communication between me and my friend at school earlier. It turned out my friend's mom had somehow heard through a mutual connection about Dad's basement business and said she no longer wanted her son to be associated with my family. It caught my mom off-guard. Her biggest fear had come true.

It was the beginning of the end for my parents' marriage. They started to argue about the situation on a regular basis. Mom reminded Dad that she knew this was going to eventually happen, and it was apparent that he was not looking to get out of the business any time soon. Dad just couldn't bring things to an end, considering the success of the business with no limit in sight. He told my mom that they had a million in cash in the basement and he couldn't just pull the plug.

During this time, Mom's two closest friends, Mary and Gloria, had recently gone through divorces and decided they were going to move down to Atlanta, Georgia to start a new life. Mary was married to one of Dad's closest friends, Jack. Mom's friends also had kids who were around my same age. Considering the situation, mom wanted a fresh start and liked the idea of moving down South to Atlanta. Dad was torn but just couldn't see winding down the business. He told Mom that he could provide us with whatever we needed if she felt moving to Atlanta was what she wanted to do. The divorce seemed to be settled pretty quick and without a lot of drama. Mom worked out a monthly amount that would allow us to live comfortably in Atlanta. They agreed I would spend summers and Christmas back in Michigan with Dad.

Mom packed our belongings in her burgundy Cadillac Seville as we made plans to hit the road down to Atlanta. It all happened so fast, and I didn't really understand what we were doing. I thought maybe it was just something temporary. My parents tried not to make it seem like a big deal to avoid upsetting me as we said our goodbyes to Dad. He kneeled down in the driveway, face-to-face with me as he told me we would see each other again very soon. As we drove off from our family house, I watched Dad fade off into the distance in the rear view mirror as he waved, standing in the driveway.

# BLACK MARBLE URN

.................

I was pulled out of my thoughts and brought back into 2008 as the captain came on the speaker system announcing our final descent into Detroit. The last time I was in Detroit was eight years prior in 2000 when I was home from San Francisco to spend some time with Dad over Christmas. As we rode the escalator down to the baggage claim, it was the first time I didn't find Dad in his usual spot waiting for me at the bottom. We had made plans to stay at my Uncle Dave and Aunt Mickey's house in Wyandotte while in town. My Uncle Dave picked us up at the airport and even though we were all going through such a rough time processing what had just happened Uncle Dave was happy to see us. Walking into his backyard brought back so many childhood memories. Their house has been in the family for over thirty years, and I have so many fond memories of family barbeque pool parties in the summer and Christmas celebrations in the winter at that house.

The next morning I met with the staff at the funeral home, and they discussed the logistics of the funeral. They had a large room reserved all afternoon and evening for everyone to gather and share stories. They also had a downstairs lounge with a kitchen for us to bring food and drinks. The coordinator asked me to provide some of my favorite photos of Dad & Jack along with a few songs for them to make a short video remembering them that could be played in the background during the gathering. I picked out some of my favorite photos from my Facebook account along with a few others that my family had and sent them to the lead coordinator. Since Rod Stewart was Dad's favorite artist, I picked Rod Stewart's "Forever Young" and Elton John's "Rocket Man" as the songs to be used in the short video. During that meeting, I looked through a catalogue of keepsakes and selected a black marble urn for Dad's ashes along with a titanium pendant that would hold a small amount of his ashes for me to keep around my neck on a chain.

The day of the funeral, I was shocked at how many people showed up. What started off as a very somber gathering gradually became what felt more like a celebration for the lives of Dad & Jack. Countless people came up to me who I had never met but had known Dad even before I was born. They wanted to introduce themselves, pay their respects, and tell me how special my dad was. They shared stories of some of their favorite memories with Dad & Jack. I was proud to introduce Jennifer as my wife to anyone who we had never met. It was great to have her with me during such an emotional day. It was a long day, with everyone congregating in the main room or downstairs in the lounge by the kitchen sharing stories with each other and catching up on old times. It became obvious from the number of people that showed up that day how much Dad & Jack were loved.

The next morning, St. Patrick's Catholic Church held a memorial Mass for Dad & Jack. I used to attend Mass at St. Patrick's with Dad when we lived together in Wyandotte back when I was a young teenager. My family had been going to that same church for generations. Being back in that church I thought about the winter when I lived with Dad when I was fifteen, and his bribe to let me drive the car home if I joined him for Mass on Sundays.

At the end of the memorial Mass, they opened up the mic for anyone who wanted to come up and say a few words in loving memory of Dad & Jack. I really wasn't in the mood to talk in front of the whole church, but something was urging me to get up. I felt Dad would've been proud, and as his only child, I felt strongly that I would regret it later if I didn't say something. I walked up to the front of the church, and considering everything that had happened, being nervous wasn't even possible. I thanked everyone for all of the love and support they had shown toward Dad & Jack over the past few days. I told a quick story about my last discussion with Dad while driving home from a trip snowboarding in California as we both loved skiing. I mentioned how special Dad was to me as my best friend. I hesitated because I didn't know if it was the right thing to say, but I proceeded to say that I just thought my dad was cool! At that moment, someone in the church screamed out a proud "Yeah!" which lightened the mood a bit and brought a smile to my face.

As the Mass came to an end, we walked out of the church and I saw that I had a voicemail. It was the funeral home letting me know they had Dad's ashes ready for me to pick up. My step-father Peter who was in town with my mom for the funeral gave me a ride to the funeral home. I walked through the door into the front office, where I was invited to take a seat. They brought out a small cardboard box and delicately handed it over to me. I remember being surprised how heavy it was, considering its size. I couldn't believe I was holding Dad's remains. It provided a little bit of comfort that he was now with me. When thinking about what I should do with Dad's ashes my first reaction was to book a trip to Vail, Colorado, ski out into the back bowls and find a beautiful place amongst the trees to place them. When we met up with Mom later that day as part of a family gathering, I told her about what I was thinking for Dad's ashes. She didn't think I should do anything with them right away and urged me to keep them with us at the house for some time before releasing them. I agreed with her, it felt like the right thing to do. I wanted Dad to be with us at our new home for a while to be around Jake as a baby.

Before heading to the airport, I had one more thing to take care of. My family had provided a recommendation to work with Tom Kuzmiak as an estate lawyer. I made an appointment to stop by his office in Wyandotte, which was only a few blocks from where I had lived with Dad when I started high school. I walked into Tom's small office, and he invited me into the conference room so we could get to know each other. I immediately felt comfortable with him; he had a calmness to him, and I liked him very much from our first meeting. He explained the process, everything that went into closing an estate, and the timeframe of it all. I provided all my basic information, and he said we would be in touch on a regular basis while we worked through everything together. I was grateful to have him engaged as he was very knowledgeable, and I had no idea where to even start. I thanked him for his time and told him we had to head to the airport to catch our flight back to California.

Uncle Dave dropped us off at the airport and we said our goodbyes know-ing I would be back shortly. While going through airport security, one of the guards asked for my ID, and in comparing my face to the picture, he joked that I looked a lot happier in my photo ID. I showed him the little box of Dad's ashes, telling him this trip wasn't a vacation and I was heading home after picking up the ashes of my dad, who passed away last week. The security guard's face went from joking to serious, and he apologized. Jenn & I made our way to the gate for our flight back to Orange County. We boarded the plane, found our seats, and took off from my hometown. As I laid my head back on the headrest and closed my eyes my mind took me back to 1981 when Mom and I had left Dad in Detroit as part of our move down to Atlanta.

# MAGIC

·················

It was a nine-hour drive from Riverview, MI to Marietta, Georgia. The drive felt like it took days and made me realize how far away we were moving away from Dad. By the time we arrived to meet Mom's friends Mary and Gloria with their kids for a celebration lunch, I was extremely upset at the whole situation. Mom explained this would be our new home and I would grow to love it in the South. Gloria and Mary had already settled into a neighborhood called the Village, which they had chosen because it was within a great public school system. In the beginning, Mom and I stayed with Gloria and her daughter Austi, who was a few years younger than me, while we looked for our own place in the neighborhood. Mom found a small two-bedroom house to rent a few houses down. Mom enrolled me to start first grade at Brumby Elementary school in the fall. Considering such a big change, it was nice to have Austi along with Mary's kids—Jason, who was four years older, and his sister Jackee, who was a year older than me—to play with. I looked up to Jason like a big brother. We spent our time going back and forth between each other's houses. We played in the local neighborhood creeks and sharks & minnows at the community pool during the summer months. It worked out well having Mary and Gloria in the neighborhood to take turns driving us to school or babysitting if needed. I became very close with Jason, Jackee, and Austi during that period, and I was starting to warm up to our new life living in the South.

After our move down to Marietta, Dad sold the house in Riverview Forest along with the Walled Lake house and bought a new house in Farmington Hills, Michigan. It was a tri-level house with a finished basement and a large backyard. It was set up as a bachelor pad with one of the first big-screen TVs, a high-end Marantz stereo system, back deck with a hot tub, and a chipping green to hit golf balls into the backyard. Dad continued to grow his businesses out of the new house with regular trips down to the Fort Lauderdale house.

Toward the end of my first year in the new school, Dad called to let mom know he was planning a trip down to Fort Lauderdale. He asked if he could stop by to see me on the trip back. He mentioned he wouldn't be able to stay long but just wanted to see me. The plan was that when Dad arrived, he would join my mom to pick me up from school. I couldn't wait for school to end that day and for him to see me walk out of my new school as a grown-up first grader. When the bell rang that day, I walked out and got excited seeing him sitting in the passenger seat of Mom's car. We headed back to the house to spend the afternoon together. I showed him my room, told him all about the new neighborhood and my new friends at school. During this period, my mom had just started hanging out with a guy named Braxton, a handsome guy who collected luxury and exotic cars. My mom had asked Braxton to stop by because she thought Dad would've like to see some of his cars. Braxton stopped by in a black-on-black two-door convertible Mercedes. Dad and Braxton hit it off over their shared interest in cars. Dad loved Braxton's Mercedes and asked if he would consider selling it. Dad made him an offer he couldn't refuse, paid in cash, and drove it back up to Michigan.

In 1982, Mom and I moved out of the small two-bedroom house we were renting and into our own three-bedroom two-story house that had a large two-car garage. It was a new construction house located on the other side of the neighborhood. Mom had the large master bedroom on the main floor, and I had the whole upstairs to myself, which included a large bedroom, bathroom, and a loft space. In the early years of living in that house, I was into ninjas and breakdancing. I had a whole ninja outfit, and I would climb out of my upstairs window and down our backyard pergola to run down to a local wooded creek area by our house to work on my ninja skills. I would practice climbing trees with my grappling hook and throw Chinese stars. When I wasn't a ninja, I was breakdancing. Mom gave me half of the garage since we only had one car, so I set up a DJ booth with a carboard dance floor to practice. I had Afrika Bambaataa's song "Plant Rock" on vinyl and loved the movies *Breakin'* & *Beat Street*. Mom had just gotten a cherry-red 944 Porsche, which she parked in the other space. The Porsche was a beautiful car, and I felt cool getting dropped off and picked up from school. Mary, Jason, and Jackee bought a house directly across the street from us, so we were always back and forth between the two houses. I started to build up a good group of friends from the neighborhood and school. I really enjoyed those years in that house and often had dreams later in my life that took place back in that house.

In 1983, Dad was out with his friends at an '80s nightclub in Detroit when he met and fell in love with a girl named Misti. He was thirty-eight at the time, and Misti was twenty. She was a thin, pretty girl with big hair and very much into '80s fashion. Dad invited Misti and her friends back to the Farmington Hills house for an after-party while the nightclub was winding down for the night. Back at the house, the '80s disco music continued on the house stereo system while Dad videoed Misti and her friends dancing, displaying them on the big-screen TV. From that night on, Dad and Misti were a couple, exposing her to a lifestyle she had never seen.

That summer, we made plans for me to stay with Dad and Misti. Back then, kids could fly solo with the supervision of the airline crew, so Mom drove me to the Atlanta airport and walked me to the gate. An assigned airline attendant escorted me to my seat and then off the plane to meet Dad at the gate in Detroit. On the drive back to the house, Dad told me about a new boat he bought, which would be arriving in a few days. He said it was a black thirty-foot offshore racer named Magic, made by a boat company called Sleekcraft out of California. He was so excited to have another boat to take family and friends out on the lake over the summer. Later that afternoon, Misti showed up at the house, and I liked her right away. She was really pretty had such a bubbly personality. Later that evening, we played dance music on the house stereo and took turns showing each other our moves. Dad mentioned he had to leave the house in the morning but would leave behind the Mercedes for Misti and I to spend the day together. I told Misti how I liked the band

Def Leppard and wanted to get a cassette tape of their album *Pyromania* to play on the house stereo. The next morning before heading off to the music store with Misti, I watched Dad walk out the door. He was talking on a large cordless phone, carrying a brown leather briefcase and his beeper was clipped on the front pocket of his jeans. I thought he looked really cool.

Later on that week Dad's boat had arrived and was down at the Wyandotte marina. Dad invited a few other friends and family members to join us for Magic's first day on the water. Everyone was so excited for a fun day out on the lake. At the marina, boats were stored in very large closed-in structures that looked like airplane hangars. Inside the structures, the boats were stored in racks from floor to ceiling and taken in and out using a forklift. There were probably a hundred boats stored in each of the two hangers. As I walked by the large front doors, I looked for Magic, but there were so many boats, it was hard to find. The hangars were so large that the boats looked like little toys in comparison. As we all waited on the dock, Dad handed out yellow-and-orange bandanas for everyone to wear to match the trim colors of Magic and make us look like a coordinated race team. We turned our attention to a forklift slowly backing out of one of the hangers and got a glimpse of the back side of a black boat with the words "Magic" in yellow and orange. As the forklift continued to slowly back out, it revealed Magic's long body, and it was an undeniably stunning boat.

The forklift turned around and set Magic in the water next to the dock where everyone was standing. The interior had black leather seating with orange-and-yellow piping. Magic was a sexy-looking boat that just looked fast! Everyone stepped into the boat with our coolers and snacks as Dad started the engines, which had a deep rumble like a hot rod. You could tell Dad was excited and absolutely in love with his new toy. We cruised around the lake for a while, listening to the roar from the engines while Dad got a feel for how the boat handled. We found a spot where there was a gathering of other boats and decided to drop the anchor and hang out for a while. We swam in the lake, flew kites off the back of Magic, and listened to '80s music while the adults enjoyed their drinks on a hot summer day with clear blue skies. When the kites crashed down into the lake, I would dive into the water and swim out to retrieve them. Later that afternoon, the crew was hungry, so we headed over to a popular restaurant on the water called Portofino's. As we pulled up alongside of the dock, everyone at the restaurant was checking out Magic. After dinner, we headed back to the hangars, gathered up all of our belongings, and the forklift took Magic out of the water to be stored until next time.

The Farmington Hills house was a party house with people constantly stopping by and Dad hosting wild parties at night. Dad's close friend Jack was always around during that time. He was the life of the party. He'd pull out the best one-liners and always had everyone laughing from his jokes. One morning, I remember walking out of my room wearing a mismatched outfit of camouflage pants and a bright yellow sweatshirt. I ran into Jack, and as he looked me up and down, he jokingly asked, "Hey, Brett, did you get dressed in the dark?"

There were many days out on Magic and regular family barbeques at Uncle Dave's backyard pool. For one of the family get togethers, I was looking forward to performing my latest breakdancing moves with my cousin Brian. At the pool party, my Uncle Rich and one of his buddies, Jimmy, challenged me and my cousin Brian to a breakdance battle. Not to be outdone by my grey & navy PUMA sweat suit with blue suede PUMA shoes, Uncle Rich and Jimmy walked out of the pool house before the battle wearing matching swim goggles. Shortly into my performance, one of my dad's drunken buddies, set his drink down, ran across the backyard, scooped me up mid-backspin, and ran into the pool holding me. My performance came to abrupt ending as I stood there, almost in tears because my new Puma suit was stretched out from being soaking wet.

# FREESTYLE BMX

....................

In 1984, I was back in Detroit for the Christmas holidays. I usually spent Christmas Eve with my dad's side of the family and Christmas Day at my grandparents' on my mom's side. My grandma Van Norman and my mom's side of the family always went big on presents. That year, my great-grandfather bought me a new bike as a surprise. Leading up to the holidays, Mom and I went to our local bike shop, called Free-flight, as I needed to get my BMX bike fixed. They had a custom chrome Haro Sport Freestyle bike in the front window. It was the coolest bike I had ever seen, and since it was custom-built, it was one of a kind. I stood there in awe looking at the bike in the front window. I told Mom how much I loved the bike while she tried to snap me back into reality, saying I already had a bike and didn't need another one. Leading up to Christmas that year, my mom told my grandma about the bike, who then mentioned it to my great-grandpa, who immediately said he wanted to buy the bike for me all on his own. I couldn't believe he bought me the bike, and I was so grateful. I would stare at it in the garage when I wasn't able to ride as I was so in love with it.

Over the next few years, bike tricks, or freestyling, became my obsession. Freestyle bikes were modified BMX bikes that had foot pegs extending the front and rear axles that could be used to stand on while doing tricks. Freestyle bikes had front and rear brakes with a mechanism that would allow the rider to spin the handlebars any which way without the brake cables getting tangled up. The possibilities of tricks on these new style of bikes was endless. The freestyle bike trend exploded in the mid '80s with the movie *Rad* being the holy grail of freestyle and BMX riding. I can't even count how many times I had watched the movie, and I spent all my free time in front of the house, working on tricks from the movie. I drove my mom crazy, making her watch a video clip of one of the pros doing a trick from the movie then making her follow me outside so I could show her that I could do the same trick. I loved the counterculture of the sport, and I always looked at the magazines to see what tricks the pros were doing, how their bikes were set up, and the clothes they were wearing. My interest in fashion was definitely something I got from Dad, and I loved the color pink during this period. Most of my idols in the BMX magazines lived in California so I associated California as a place where cool people live. I became close with a local group of kids from my school, who had freestyle bikes and were also into the sport. I started hanging out a lot with one of the kids, Joe, who lived a short ride away across the main road in a different neighborhood. We were always meeting up at a designated spot in one of the local neighborhoods to practice tricks or play bike tag, which was like tag only on bikes. The faster and better you were at handling your bike, the harder you were to catch. We were always on our bikes, progressing very quickly in the sport, striving to impress each other and become known as one of the best riders around. From my obsession and countless hours practicing, I got pretty good at the sport.

In 1985, Dad was planning to attend a large sporting expo in Atlanta and reserved booth space to promote TeeWizz. While telling me about the expo, he mentioned that he had extra passes for me and a friend to attend one of the days. He asked Mom and Gloria if they would be interested in hanging around at the expo as a couple of pretty booth girls to draw people into discussions about TeeWizz. Mom and Gloria were two pretty blondes who turned heads wherever they went, so they were perfect. After I asked around, one of my friends, Keith, wanted to join me for a day at the expo. Keith was part of our bike gang, though he was more of a football player. He was a good-looking athletic kid who was half-black and half-white. As we walked into the expo, it became apparent how big of an event it was with all the major sporting brands in attendance. Dad had a box of these clear plastic neckties that had various golf-inspired emblems inside them and asked if we wanted to wear them while walking around as a conversation piece for TeeWizz. They looked silly to me, so I didn't wear one, but Keith wore one proudly all day.

During the afternoon, I was walking around by myself when I was stopped dead in my tracks in disbelief as I walked by Converse's large sprawling booth. Right there in front of me were two of my favorite freestyle riders—Ron Wilkerson and Dennis McCoy from the magazines—just hanging out on their bikes in their full riding gear. I had to introduce myself but was so starstruck I could barely talk. Ron Wilkerson told me they were just about to start their show as everyone starting forming a big circle around them. Freestyle shows were kind of similar to breakdancing with one person performing while everyone else stood in a circle around watching. I couldn't believe I was actually watching my idols perform their tricks live as opposed to seeing them in magazines or videos. After the show, the circle closed in on them, and they were bombarded with people, so I decided to head back to the TeeWizz booth to tell everyone about it.

Walking back across the expo, I saw a large performance going on at one of the booths that looked like some kind of dance party with music blasting and a bunch of people dancing on a stage. As I walked by, I saw Keith dancing with a bunch of girls on the stage as if he was part of the performance. He saw me and got down from the stage to come talk to me as he could tell I was excited about something. I told him all about the pros at the Converse booth, and we exchanged stories while walking back to the TeeWizz booth. I told my mom and dad all about it, and they could tell how excited I was from the experience. Mom told me David Hasselhoff stopped by the TeeWizz booth and took a picture with her and Gloria. It was a fun event, and we all had a great time.

After the expo, Dad hung around for a few days meeting some of my other friends. We all got together in front of our house to show Dad all of our bike tricks. It was during this time when our local roller-skating rink, called Sparkles, became a popular place, and our school often sponsored skate nights. I loved going to Sparkles and tried to go as often as possible. I loved skating around to '80s music and flirting with the pretty girls from our school. Dad took me and a group of my friends to Sparkles while he was still in town and had a blast with us.

Later that year, my Haro Sport was stolen from the backyard of Mary, Jason, and Jackee's house. After spending the night at their house, I came out in the morning to ride home, and my bike was nowhere to be found. I felt such a rush of panic and disbelief that the thing I loved most was gone. I couldn't believe someone came in through a closed gate and around to the back of the house to steal it. Analyzing everything, I wondered if someone had been watching me take it in through the gate and plotting. When I got home and told Mom, she was absolutely furious! I was so upset with myself. I felt like I had been taken advantage of, and it drove me crazy to think someone was out there riding around on my bike like it was now their own.

Mom was ready to scour the earth to find it, and I had no choice to follow along. Deep down inside, I felt it was hopeless. We spent hours driving around from neighborhood to neighborhood, looking all over to hopefully find some kid riding it around, and those days in the car with her were so uncomfortable. Then one day about a month later, my friend Keith saw another kid hanging out in his neighborhood on my bike. Keith immediately walked up to the kid and told him, "Get off my boy's bike, or I'm gonna beat your ass." The kid wanted no part of Keith, so he got off the bike and handed it over. Keith's mom drove him over to my house with my bike in the back of their car. Keith walked my bike up to the house, knocked on the door, and when my mom answered, Keith said, "Hi, Ms. Langley. Here's Brett's bike back." I was away from the house at the time, but when I came back, my mom told me what had happened and said my bike was back in the garage. I headed toward with an overwhelming sense of relief and happiness that I had my prized possession back.

Not long after, it was late and I was heading home with Joe after riding bikes all day. Powers Ferry was the main road back to our neighborhoods which was a long steep downhill ride. One of the lanes was closed off at the time for some road construction. Joe and I were flying down the road on our bikes inside the closed off section. This was before anyone wore helmets or bike lights were a thing. I was riding in front of Joe and didn't see a car that suddenly turned in front of us into a neighborhood entrance right as we were about to cross. I slammed into the front side of the car by the wheel. It happened so quick I wasn't sure what had happened. The next thing I remember was the lady driving had screamed at the situation while I was lying on the hood of the car with the back of my head on the windshield. Once I came to my senses, the adrenaline kicked in, and I quickly got off the side of the car. My initial thought was to get out of there, but when I grabbed my bike, it was clear that it was unrideable from the crash. Joe and the lady kept asking if I was ok, but all I could think about was Mom finding out about the situation and how much trouble I was going to be in.

Before I knew it, there was an ambulance at the scene, and they asked my name, my mother's name, and my home phone number. I told them I was fine and begged them not to call my mom. The ambulance driver told me she was going to be happy that I was ok, which comforted me a bit. At this point, I had given into the process, gave them my information, and got into the ambulance. Joe told me that he would take my bike back to his house and I could get it later. Mom met me at the hospital. After being checked out by the doctor, I only had minor cuts and bruises from the crash. Mom could tell I was pretty shaken up from the experience, so she was very calm and comforting as we checked out of the hospital.

# CALM CANOE POND

·····················

After the flight home from the funeral, we were back at our little house in our neighborhood Canoe Pond. We had only lived in the house a little over 3 months, but it was nice to have our own place during such a difficult time in my life. I was still trying to process the whole situation and how to move forward. I was looking for signs from Dad that he was in a better place. Elton John's "Rocket Man" kept coming on in the most random places and times and made me think it was Dad letting me know that he was with me. Outside of handling everything going on with Dad, the news continued to be a constant stream of negativity being in the early phases of the 2008 financial crisis. The only thing keeping me together was the love and support from Jennifer and having our son Jake at the house. I had requested to take some time off from work, as an Account Executive for a large software company, because I just wasn't in a place mentally where I could focus on sales prospecting. As a gift, my company had sent me a wind chime, which I hung up in our little back-yard area. It provided a soothing sound at the house whenever the wind blew.

The black marble urn I ordered for Dad's ashes arrived at the house. It felt good to get them out of the cardboard box and into a nice urn. I placed the urn and a large framed picture of Dad from our wedding in the built-in bookcase next to our TV. Jake was only about seven months old, so Jenn and I kept the house pretty quiet as he was constantly in and out of naps. When I could, I would head to the beach early mornings to surf. Being submerged in the cold ocean for an hour followed by a hot shower back at the house was something that helped to calm my nerves.

I was calling the detectives back in Riverview often, but they weren't telling me anything new or substantial. It had been a few weeks since what took place at Dad's house, and they were almost ready to turn the house over to me. I booked my flight back to the Detroit and scheduled some time to meet with my estate lawyer while in town. I packed my bags to spend a couple days back in Detroit. Jenn & Jake dropped me back off at the airport. I made my way through the Orange County airport, boarded the plane and found my seat against the window. As we took off and I stared out the window. I thought about the summer of 1986 that I spent with Dad & Misti in a Costa Mesa townhouse close by to where Jenn & I ended up starting our family all those years later.

# LATE '80S TRANSITIONS

..................

It was early 1986 when things went south for Dad's marijuana operations. During one of the usual trips down to Miami, one of his drivers had coordinated a side hustle to pick up a large amount of cocaine and bring back up to Detroit to sell on his own. It turned out that the cocaine contact in Miami was an undercover federal agent. Luckily, through one of his connections, Dad heard the news while the driver was on the road back up to Detroit. The feds had planned to arrest Dad at the drop-off point in Detroit, but Dad never showed up. It was from this point on that Dad knew he would be watched and was done with his marijuana business.

As the summer approached, Dad made plans for me to spend the summer with he and Misti. Considering the situation, Dad wanted to get out of Detroit for a little while. He told me that we were going to spend the summer in California as he was in the process of moving his manufacturing operations for TeeWizz out to Laguna Niguel in Southern California. I was excited to spend the summer in California where most of the bike and skateboard pros that I admired lived. Dad told me we would be taking a road trip with Misti across the country, visiting a bunch of places along the way.

When I landed in Detroit, the three of us spent the night at the Farmington Hills house and hit the road in Dad's white Cadillac Eldorado early the next morning. We made pretty quick time through Chicago and Omaha, but once we hit the Rockies, we slowed things down, spending a couple of days at some of the western destinations. We stopped in Vail, Colorado, enjoying all the shops and restaurants in the little ski town. We took the chairlift up to the top of the mountain to do some sightseeing and hiked around, taking in the view. I had only skied Boyne Mountain in Michigan at this point in my life, so it completely opened up my mind to the size of the mountains out west. I loved the whole vibe of the Vail village during the summer.

We left Vail and made our way through Zion National Park in Utah, which was a beautiful mountainous part of the country to drive through. We stopped for a few days at the Grand Canyon and took a helicopter ride through the canyon. We stopped in Las Vegas, walking up and down the strip and checking out all of the shops and casinos. We eventually made it to Costa Mesa, California, where we checked into a local motel close by the townhouse that we would be moving into within a few days. The townhouse was located in between the South Coast Plaza Mall and the Orange County fairgrounds. The weather was perfect every day in the mid-eighties, and our motel room was right next to the pool. We spent the next few days with the door open, playing music while Dad and Misti sat by the pool with cocktails. It was while watching the movie *Back to the Future* in our room after swimming that I wanted to get a skateboard to ride around for the summer. The next day, we took a short drive to Newport Beach. Traffic was backed up heading south on the 55 from everyone heading to the beach on such a gorgeous day. We walked the boardwalk with everyone else biking, skateboarding, roller-skating and the sound of waves crashing off the coast.

We walked by a surf shop called PJ's Surfrider on the boardwalk, and I became excited seeing the skateboards in the window. Dad knew I wasn't going to let us just walk by, so he took me inside. He let me pick out a board from the many options hanging on the wall behind the counter, and I was drawn to a stained Red Vision Mark Gonzales. With the recommendations from the guys at the shop, I had them build it up with white trucks and wheels. They did a custom grip tape job on the top where they tore the sheet of black grip tape into 5 or 6 large pieces and placed them on top of the board leaving small lines across the top where you could see the red color from the board. While they built up my skateboard, I walked around the shop, checking out all of the cool surf & skate clothes asking Dad if I could get some skate clothes. I changed at the shop into my new turquoise Maui and Son's T-shirt, khaki-colored chino beach shorts, and a Navy pair of Vans shoes. I felt like a local surfer or skater as I walked out of the shop with my new board under my arm. As we drove back from the beach later that day I had my window down, we drove by the Pacific Amphitheater, and you could hear cheering and live music off in the distance from a local concert. I immediately loved the California beach lifestyle.

Within a few days of arriving in Costa Mesa, we were able to check out of the motel and move into our townhouse. It was a two-story three-bedroom layout with a small back patio. We spent our days exploring the coastal beach towns, shopping at South Coast Plaza, and hanging around the community pool in our complex. I loved skating around the complex, which had walkways that connected the different sections of the neighborhood. Early in the summer, Dad mentioned how he had always admired people who could play an instrument, and it was something he wished he would have started earlier in life. He asked me if I had any interest in learning an instrument, and guitar came to mind as something that would be cool to be able to play. Dad & I took a trip over to the Guitar Center in Fountain Valley. Like the skate shop, there were so many guitars on the wall to choose from. I gravitated toward this black Stratocaster style of guitar, and the store recommended a small Fender practice amp to start with. Dad signed me up for lessons, and I began practicing in between skateboarding around the neighborhood and trips to the beach.

One morning, I was woken up to an unusual feeling of my bedroom shaking. The furniture rattled around. It had woken me up from a deep sleep, so I wasn't sure if it was a dream or why the room was pulsating. Dad ran into the room and frantically grabbed me out of bed, making his way down the stairs with me hunched over his shoulder before the shaking stopped. As he turned around to head back upstairs, Misti was sitting up in bed and visibly upset that Dad's immediate instinct was to grab me and head outside. Dad tried to explain himself to Misti, saying he thought she was right there with him, but she was still upset. It was a scary experience. None of us had ever been through that, living in Detroit or Atlanta.

At the end of the summer, it was time for me to head back to Marietta, Georgia, to start school in the fall. Dad booked a direct flight for me from Los Angeles to Atlanta. Dad and Misti drove me up to the LA airport and checked me into my flight. An airline attendant greeted us at the gate, I hugged Dad and Misti goodbye, and was escorted to my seat. The flight crew watched over me during the flight, and then escorted me off the flight to meet my Mom.

It was shortly after this that the investigators had sufficient evidence to bring Dad into court, and it was time for him to face the music back in Detroit. Dad wrapped things up on the Costa Mesa townhouse, selling off the furniture, and he and Misti hit the road back to Detroit. Once they were back in town, the focus was on his court case. The situation put a strain on their relationship. Misti moved in with her parents while Dad moved in with my Aunt Cathy and her husband, Mark, while things got sorted out.

Dad hired a strong attorney, and it seemed as the prosecutors didn't have substantial evidence that tied Dad to dealing marijuana. They focused on trying to relate Dad's financial success to dealing, but the hard evidence just wasn't there. Dad was smart in how he set up his operations, and once he stopped the deals, there wasn't much for the police to go by. Toward the end of the trial they brought in my mom, Misti, and another girl "Chatty Cathy", who was a girlfriend of Jimmy, one of Dad's closest friends. Chatty Cathy got the nickname because she was shy and didn't talk much. All three took the stand to field questions about their relationship with Dad and their understanding of his business, but they didn't have much to say as Dad did a good job keeping things under the radar. In the end, Dad was charged with tax evasion and sentenced to three years in a federal prison.

Prior to the trial, Dad liquidated all of his assets and put some money aside for the next chapter in his life. As part of Dad's sentence, the lawyer was able to negotiate for him to serve his time in a minimum security prison in Minnesota, which was mainly for white-collar criminals. It could hardly be considered a place where one goes to serve hard time. Dad pleaded with Misti to wait for him while he was away, but she felt she was too young to wait three years, so they had broken off their engagement. Dad was absolutely heartbroken as he was crazy about Misti. The separation would only make things harder for him while he was gone.

It was time for Dad to break the news to me that we wouldn't be able to see each other for our normal visits during Christmas and the summers. He explained to me that he had to leave the country for a few years as he was moving his manufacturing of TeeWizz to Taiwan and needed to be there to support the business. He told me that we would be able to write each other letters and talk over the phone every so often. I was heartbroken that it was going to be such a long period before I would see him again. Once Dad had all his affairs in order, with some cash set aside, he flew from Detroit to Minnesota and checked himself into the facility to serve his sentence.

Mom knew the situation since she had been involved in the trial. It was obvious that Dad's financial situation had changed dramatically, and the large monthly checks would be coming to an end. Mom became focused on downsizing our monthly expenses. She traded in her Red Porsche 944 for a more practical used Cadillac Cimarron. She sold our house in the Village, rolling the equity into a smaller house on the other side of town, which provided a lower monthly payment. She got a full-time job at a retail clothing store called Rich's, which was a department store based in the Southeast. Mom worked in the women's high-end fashion department. Her employee discount allowed her to get a good discount on school clothes for me as Rich's had a boys' department.

With Mom working long hours, I had to keep myself entertained after school until she came home. Since moving to the other side of town and away from my friends, I spent most of my time outside of school working on new bike tricks in front of the house or playing *Zelda* and *Metroid* on my Nintendo gaming system. My daily routine in sixth grade consisted of taking the bus to school and home in the afternoon. After school, I would let myself into the house, practice tricks out front until dark, make dinner (which was usually a TV dinner, Swedish meatballs, or MicroMagic French fries), and then watch

Dial MTV, which would show the top ten music videos based on the fans' dial-in requests for the day. That year was a big year for Def Leppard's "Pour Some Sugar on Me" as it consistently dominated the charts. Being home alone after dark, I was scared to sleep upstairs in my bed, so I would fall asleep on the couch downstairs with the TV on for comfort. When Mom got home around 9:00 p.m., she would wake me up to go sleep in my bed.

During that year, I had received my first letter from Dad, and we started sending letters back and forth. In the beginning of the school year, I wrote mostly about my progress on my bike, but toward the end of the year, I had started to gravitate more toward skateboarding with the release of Powell Peralta's *The Search for Animal Chin*. The movie was based on a group of professional skateboarders called the Bones Brigade, who set out skating around the country in search for this mythical skater named Animal Chin. My whole group of bike friends became hooked on that movie, and soon enough, bikes became skateboards, and we all had a new set of challenges in front of us as we now wanted to excel in skateboarding.

After sixth grade, Mom sold our house, and we downsized into a smaller townhouse back on the other side of town which was closer to the Village where I spent all of my elementary school years. My passion for skateboarding was through the roof, and now that I was closer to my friends, we were skating distance away from meeting up. We spent all of our time outside of school seeking undiscovered spots to skate and hunting for backyard ramps.

We studied all the skate videos, trying to learn all of the new tricks and copied the clothing trends of our favorite pro skaters. To me style was a big component of skateboarding. If you took two skaters who could both do the same trick but one of them had a unique style when they did the same trick it just looked cooler. Skateboarding was an extension of someone's individual taste that included the way they dressed and the music they listened to. Even the board someone chose to skate and how they set it up was a reflection of their own style. During this time is when I became attracted to hip-hop. I felt it went hand in hand with skateboarding as they were both cutting edge art forms that went perfect together. I loved Public Enemy's album *It Takes A Nation of Millions To Hold Us Back* and it was my favorite music to skate to during this period.

It was within a few months of Mom and I moving into our townhouse that she was set up on a blind date with a guy named Peter Spirer, who was quite a bit older. He was the CEO of Horizon Carpets, which was the third largest carpet manufacturing company in the world. Peter also owned a local high-end nightclub called Scenario's where a lot of the successful business crowd and young pretty girls hung out. Peter was previously married and had two sons and a daughter who were all considerably older than me. The blind date was set up for Mom to meet Peter at Scenario's, and there was an immediate attraction between them. They became inseparable from that night on, and Peter started to become a regular figure in our lives. Peter was a world traveler and started taking Mom with him on his business trips, exposing her to a life she had never seen before.

One of Mom's friends, who she worked with at Rich's, was a young woman in her early twenties named Cameron who started staying with me at the townhouse while Mom and Peter traveled. There were times when they were out of the country for a few weeks at a time. Cameron looked like she was straight out of an '80s glam rock video with big hair, ripped jeans and white high-top sneakers. She drove a little red Honda CRX, and my friends were always in awe when she would drop me off at school or take me to skate somewhere. I liked to pretend it wasn't a big deal that I was hanging out with this pretty, older girl. Hanging out with Cameron kind of felt like the scenario in the '80s movie *Weird Science* where the two main characters, who were high school kids, created a fantasy girl on their computer and through an association with her it helped with their popularity amongst their peers. Cameron took me where ever I wanted to go for skateboarding, we got along really well, and had a lot of fun together.

One day while out in front of the townhouse skating, I stopped by our mailbox to find a letter from Dad. I always loved getting letters from him, so I headed inside to read through it. In the past, I never paid much attention to the return address but started to wonder why it had a Minnesota address. I thought maybe that was the post office where the letters were coming through from Taiwan, but it was Dad's handwriting. In the letter, Dad mentioned he wanted to talk and would be calling the house over the next few days. I always loved our phone conversations to hear his voice. Anytime the phone would ring, I was filled with excitement. I answered the phone one evening, and it was him. For our conversation, he mainly just listened to me talk about my skateboarding. Toward the end of our call, I asked about the Minnesota return address, which caused him to pause, but then he proceeded to tell me he was no longer in Taiwan. He told me that he was in a hospital located in Minnesota because he wanted to stop drinking and he was in there to get healthy. I didn't really understand but was happy to hear that he was trying to take better care of himself. I asked if I could come see him, and he said not right away but he would look into it further to find a good time for me to visit.

It wasn't much longer before Dad had arranged for me to fly up to Detroit where I would be taking a road trip with my Uncle Rich, Aunt Cathy, and Aunt Denise to Minnesota. We would be traveling in a van that had a couch/bed and a mini-kitchen. The trip from Detroit to Rochester, Minnesota, was about a nine-hour drive. During our trip, I mainly just stared out the window, looking forward to seeing Dad. We arrived in Minnesota and checked into a hotel the night before we were scheduled to visit Dad at what I expected to be a hospital.

We woke up early in the morning to get ready to head to the facility. When we pulled into the parking lot, it wasn't what I had expected as it looked like a large compound with tall barbed wire fence all around the perimeter. The property had rolling grass hills and a basketball court. We entered the facility and made our way through what seemed to be a very strict security check-in process. I began to realize that it wasn't a hospital and I didn't care, I just wanted to see Dad. We were escorted by a security guard, who lead us into a large room with a bunch of small tables and chairs where a bunch of other people were visiting with each other.

After we waited at a table, Dad was escorted in wearing a black polo shirt, dark jeans, and white tennis shoes. I ran over and hugged him as tight as I could. I remember thinking that he looked muscular like he had been lifting weights. Sitting down at the table, Dad told us how he was in the best shape of his life, working out, playing basketball in the summer and hockey in the winter, and he even had a part-time job as a dental assistant in the facility. He got excited, almost like he had a secret and proceeded to tell us how Bob Probert from the Detroit Red Wings was in the facility, and he played with him as part of the winter hockey group. My family are huge Detroit sports fans, they were fans of his, and he was known as one of the toughest brawlers in the NHL. Dad told us how he was able to get a picture with him and their group out on the ice in the facility during the winter. I asked about his room, and Dad described it as being like a small apartment. He said he had a roommate, but we weren't able to leave the visiting area.

I asked how much longer he needed to stay at the facility, and he said probably another year or so but quickly changed the discussion, asking me about school and how my skateboarding was coming along. I told him I couldn't wait for him to see me skate, and he asked if I had brought my board with me. I told him my board was out in the van. Dad said he would ask if he could maybe head out into the courtyard to watch me through the fence if I wanted to show him some tricks out in the parking lot as we headed out. Dad went to talk with one of the security guards and came back to the table, saying he could watch me from the courtyard briefly at the end of visiting hours, which were almost over. As we started saying our goodbyes, I started crying as I didn't want to leave him. Dad tried to cheer me up by saying how much he couldn't wait to see me skate and that we would see each other soon.

By the time we arrived back out at the van, I could see Dad standing off in the distance in the courtyard, ready to watch. I was pretty emotional about the whole situation but still wanted to show Dad my tricks. My family leaned up against the side of the van to watch. I skated back and forth in front of the fence, showcasing all of the tricks I had been working on at the time. After I had run through all of them a few times, I stopped to say my final goodbye, waving with my board under the other arm. I could see Dad clapping off in the distance, and then he waved goodbye. We loaded back into the van to make our way back to Detroit. As we drove off, I saw Dad fade off into the distance, reminding of me when Mom and I had left for Atlanta. I thought about him the whole drive back to Detroit and on my flight back down to Atlanta. I couldn't stop thinking about how much I wanted to be with him once he was out of that facility and back in Detroit.

Once back in Atlanta, I told Mom all about the trip and how strong I felt about wanting to be there for Dad when he was released from the facility. Mom didn't like what she was hearing about my desire to move back to Detroit to live with him. She said, "Your Dad is in prison for selling drugs." I knew the situation at this point and wanted to give him the benefit of the doubt. I loved my Dad and didn't feel he had done anything wrong. He was a cool, easy going guy who was fun to be around and extremely generous to others. He didn't have a mean bone in his body and would never do anything to hurt or harm anyone. I felt being there with him as he started a new chapter in his life would be a positive thing. Mom & I started to argue about the situation on a regular basis. She would often say how much I was like my dad. She felt I had so much more to gain growing up under the influence of Peter as a father figure and role model, considering his success.

Mom and I started to spend more time living at Peter's townhouse, which was in the upscale area in Atlanta called Buckhead. Peter's luxury townhouse was filled with contemporary artwork as he was a well-known art collector in Atlanta. The townhouse had a piano, a large wine cellar, and a downstairs safari-themed room with a stone jacuzzi and sauna room. It had shiny gold mirror handrails on the staircase that you weren't supposed to touch as it would leave fingerprints. It was right next to the prestigious private school Lovett, and discussions started about how it would be a great school for me to attend.

Peter & I laughed for years about a story from that townhouse when one morning I was up early and stepped out the front door to check the weather for skating that day. Being as quiet as I could, I cracked open the front door, but I set off the security alarm. Considering how loud it was, I was instantly filled with panic and unsure how to stop it. As I ran back into the house to make my way back up the stairs, Peter came barreling down the stairs the other way, wearing nothing but a T-shirt of one of his favorite artists that covered half his belly and nothing else. The sight of Peter only added to the shock of the whole situation as we stood face-to-face on the stairs, him asking me what happened. I could see his mouth moving but couldn't hear anything he was saying over the alarm. The fact that he was naked from the waist down didn't seem to matter to him as he was focused on figuring out what had happened. He went and turned the alarm off, and it was fair to say we were all awake. It was kind of like an icebreaker in my relationship with Peter as I felt like I knew him better after that moment.

Peter wanted Mom and I to experience all the city had to offer. We started having dinners out at Atlanta's finest restaurants. It was all such a big change from not that long ago when Mom and I were living in our small townhouse just getting by.

In my next letter to Dad, I wrote about my feelings and how I wanted to live with him once he was out of the facility. I mentioned the arguments with Mom and how things were on track for us to move in with Peter. After Dad received my letter, he mentioned my desire to move back up to Detroit to my family. My Aunt Cathy told my dad that if I wanted, she and my Uncle Mark would love for me to stay with them until he was released from the facility. In my dad's follow-up letter, he mentioned that I could stay with my aunt and uncle for my eighth grade year until his release, which was anticipated just after I would start my freshman year of high school. I immediately knew that was what I wanted to do as it put me on a path of being with Dad once he was out. Mom wasn't happy with the whole situation, but she knew it was something I felt strongly about, and she allowed me to make my own decision.

I relocated up to Rochester Hills, Michigan, to move in with Aunt Cathy, Uncle Mark, and their two little kids, Ashley and Kyle. Rochester Hills is a nice upscale area about forty minutes away from where I was born in Wyandotte. They welcomed me with open arms into their home. They are such a wonderful family that I love very much. Ashley was five, Kyle was three, and it was fun for me to have younger siblings to play with experiencing what it was like to be like an older brother. Ashley was a sweet little girl, and Kyle was a funny little kid who always kept us entertained. Once situated, I was excited to start exploring new skate spots around my new town. Aunt Cathy enrolled me in West Middle School for eighth grade, and the school was a short walking distance right across the street.

My first day of school, I walked in focused on finding a group of skaters, looking for anyone wearing skate-branded clothing. I immediately saw a group of kids wearing Powell Peralta T-shirts, introduced myself as being new to the school, and asked if they wanted to skate after school sometime. I brought my board with me to school the next day, and we met in front of the school at the end of the day. Our school had a small staircase outside the front doors down to the front pickup area. As soon as we all started skating, I earned immediate respect by ollieing down the front staircase with ease and was one of the best skaters at my new school.

It was a few months later while I was exploring new spots skating around town that I ran into an older group of high school skaters. After a session skating with them, they mentioned they had their own skate team and asked me to join. It was a great scenario as they could drive, and I got to tag along with them to all the best skate spots. We ventured to skate parks hours away and even spent a day a concrete skate park in Sarnia Canada on the other side of the bridge.

Aunt Cathy and Uncle Mark took great care of me and were very supportive of my passion for skateboarding. Uncle Mark used to look out the front window of the house and admire my dedication to the sport. He respected my drive as I spent hours upon hours on the street in front of the house, working on the same trick over and over until I finally was able to pull it off. He loved catching my reaction when I finally landed a new trick for the first time. Over the years, I gravitated toward bikes and skateboards because I liked how I could work on things by myself without needing a team to practice. Whatever I put into it was what I got out of it, and my passion for these types of activities fueled my drive to get really good at them in a relatively short amount of time. It was in early 1990 when I had reached my peak in skateboarding.

Dad was given his release date, which would be about a month after the start of my freshman year of high school in the fall of 1990. Dad told me that he was planning to move back to Wyandotte and had everything set up for me to stay with my grandma and grandpa until he was home. He mentioned how he would join me shortly after I had started school that year, and we would figure out the plan for moving into our own house. Dad wanted me to go to a better high school than the public school he had attended when he was my age. He had my family help to get me enrolled at Gabriel Richard Catholic High School located in Riverview, Michigan. My cousins Brian and Marty would be attending the same school, so my Aunt Lily and Uncle Rich helped to get me all set up to start school in the fall.

During the summer after eighth grade, I moved into the upstairs loft at my grandparents' house where Dad had grown up. In the move to Wyandotte, I didn't find much of a skate scene, and my passion started to fade. I started playing basketball with my cousin Brian and fell in love with the sport. I had found a new passion and something I wanted to get good at, so my time on a skateboard started to diminish, and my focus transitioned to basketball. I liked how even though basketball was a team sport I could practice on my own, working on my shot and ballhandling skills. My cousin Brian was really good, and he taught me the basic fundamentals on his basketball hoop on the garage. Brian and I were the exact same age, both born on the same day. He had grown up his whole life in Wyandotte and introduced me to his group of friends; some of which would be attending Gabriel Richard with us in the fall. During that summer, the city of Wyandotte had invested in the build-out of two new basketball courts at our local Polaski Park. They were side-by-side full courts that had double-rimmed hoops with painted free throw and three-point lines. They were beautiful courts and only about a twenty-minute walk from my grandma's house. People came from all over the greater Detroit area to play on the new courts. I fell in love with the whole vibe in playing in outdoor pickup games. My idols became the Detroit Pistons, aka the Bad Boys, who became back-to-back NBA champs and to me were the kings of Detroit.

That summer, I spent countless hours at the park, working on my game and trying to improve as quickly as possible. I loved all the competitive trash talk that came along with the game and how there was always rap music playing through a car stereo at the courts. I would walk over to the park in the morning, dribbling down the sidewalk listening to my rap music through headphones looking forward to playing in the fast paced games out in the sun. On the way to the park I would swing by 7-Eleven and pick up a large Gatorade as a drink for the day. Whenever I had enough, I would head back to the house; Grandma loved to cook for me whenever I was hungry.

One of my favorite stories about my grandparents was a day when Grandpa took their silver Oldsmobile Cutlass over to the local car wash. It was a beautiful summer afternoon as Grandpa backed out of the driveway while Grandma sat on the porch, enjoying the nice weather with a cold glass of lemonade. Grandpa arrived at the car wash and exited the car once it was in position to go through the automated wash. As customers head inside to pay they could watch their cars make their way through the car wash from the large interior windows. Grandpa was distracted while inside making small talk with the staff, probably telling them all about how his son Dennis went all the way with a kick return touchdown during one of his high school football games. After paying he headed out front where a silver car was running with the door open ready to be driven off. He jumped in, and on the drive back to the house noticed the radio had been changed from his usual sports station. He figured out how to adjust it back, thinking one of the car wash staff members must had bumped into the radio changing the station as part of the interior cleaning. He pulled in the driveway with Grandma still on the porch. As he got out, Grandma stood up and said, "Leo...that's not our car!"

Grandpa stood there confused in his plaid slacks, wifebeater undershirt, and newsboy hat and looked at the car next to him to figure out what she was talking about. The reality set in that it was someone else's silver car, so he quickly got back inside and drove back to the car wash. When he arrived, he tried to make light of the situation with the staff and the owner of the car standing out front. Everyone laughed at the situation as they knew it was an honest mistake. Outside of the wash, Grandpa's silver Oldsmobile Cutlass was waiting for him with the door open. He hopped in and drove back to the house, with his usual sports station already on the radio.

I loved dinner time with Grandma and Grandpa. I often thought about how Dad must have sat around the same little round table with them in their tiny kitchen when he was my age. Grandma always had a soft spot in her heart for me. I think maybe it was because she didn't see me as often as my other cousins since my parents had split up at such a young age, and I had moved away from Wyandotte. She was always in my corner, so if Grandpa started to give me a hard time about the way I dressed, my hair, or my gold hoop earring, Grandma would always jump in on my behalf. Grandma wore the pants in the house, so if she spoke up, Grandpa took the back seat. Grandpa always loved to talk about his proud moments, like watching my dad excel in football and ice speed skating in high school. The three of us were so excited for Dad to be back home.

# THE GUCCI WATCH

........................

I was brought back to the reality of 2008 with the captain coming over the speaker system announcing our final descent into the Detroit airport. During these final moments of the flight I started to get nervous as I knew I was getting close to seeing Dad's house for the first time only a few weeks after everything that had happened. The police had completed their investigation and I was able to enter the house the next morning.

My Uncle Dave picked me up at the airport late in the evening. We headed back to he and Aunt Mickey's house so I could get some rest before heading over to Dad's house in the morning. My Uncle Dave had recommended a friend of the family, a guy named Tony, who was a contractor, to join me at the house as he had a lot of experience rebuilding damaged houses. Uncle Dave thought that he would be helpful in case I had any questions. I took him up on the recommendation, and everything was coordinated for Tony to meet me at Dad's house.

The next morning when I arrived, everything hit me like a ton of bricks seeing the condition of Dad's house in person. Tony told me he was there if I needed anything, but was going to wait out front in the car to let me have some time alone in the house. The roof of the garage was completely gone from the fire. The side door in the driveway next to the garage was boarded up. That was the door Dad always used and most likely the door he entered the house the night he was attacked. I stood there for a moment, taking in the condition of the exterior of the house before entering in the front door.

The house had an overwhelming smell of smoke and mold. The pure white interior was a discolored gray from all the smoke that filled the house the night of the fire. I walked slowly through the house, taking it all in while having flashbacks of the last few times I was there during Christmas with Dad back in 1999 and 2000. I made my way to the garage, slowly walking through the foyer area where Dad did all his paperwork. Seeing the inside of the boarded up side door, I imagined what took place when Dad came through the door that night. I kept seeing that image from my dream of the look on his face when he was surprised by the intruders. I couldn't believe the damage done to that foyer area, which was just inside the garage. As I approached the garage, the sight of Dad's beautiful early '90s white Cadillac burnt down to raw metal and the roof of the car caved in from the garage roof that had collapsed onto it from the fire was overwhelming. The fire had been so strong that the wheels looked as though they had melted into the concrete garage floor. I scanned around the garage with chills, thinking about what took place the night of the crime only a few weeks earlier.

Over in the corner, there was another door with direct access into the garage by the safe that was ripped out. I could see my black 1987 Haro Master Freestyle bike that Dad had saved all these years completely mangled and destroyed from the fire. The garage floor was covered with charred vending parts, broken CDs, and a burnt TeeWizz. I stood where Dad's body was found based on the information the police had provided and said a prayer to him, hoping that he was in a better place. As I finished my prayer, I looked up through the completely open garage roof into the sky imagining him looking down on me.

After spending a considerable amount of time just standing there in the garage in shock, I walked back into the house. In the living room, there was still a large framed photo of me from high school on a console table behind the couch. The DVDs of the movies *Blow* and *Vanilla Sky* that I had sent as Christmas gifts a few years prior were next to the TV in the media cabinet.

Walking into the kitchen, I was disturbed to see the completely white kitchen turned gray from smoke. On the counter, I saw the coffee cups, glassware, and plates that Dad & Jack had used their last day in the house together. I kept thinking about a photo I took during Christmas at the house in 2000 the last time I was there. It featured my friend Jay with his arm around Dad in the kitchen as they played cards with Jack and my Uncle Bob. I headed upstairs to Dad's and Jack's bedrooms. I looked into Jack's room. It had a sliding glass door to the upstairs balcony, though it was boarded up, I assumed from the gunshots fired off in the room that shattered the glass. The room was dark with no natural light coming in considering the boarded up sliding glass door. I walked into Dad's white bedroom, and like the other rooms in the house, it was pretty much completely discolored and destroyed from all the smoke. Dad's bathroom still had his daily toiletries sitting on the counter that he used his final day in the house. There was an open and empty Ruger gun case by the closet that Dad had for home protection. I wondered what happened to the gun. Did the intruders find it and use it that night, did they take it with them when they left the house or did the police have it as evidence. I wondered what would have happened if Dad would have gotten to the gun first that night.

I was really hoping to find this brown crocodile band Gucci watch that I had bought for Dad a few years prior to take home with me as a family keepsake. I bought him the watch as a gift to show my appreciation for everything that he had done for me over the years once I had started to experience some financial success in my career. I looked through all of his dresser drawers along with any place where he may have kept it but no luck. I figured the intruders took it while they cleaned out the house of anything valuable the night of the crime. I was disappointed because it really was the only thing I really wanted to retrieve from the house as it had a lot of sentimental value to me. I headed down to the basement. Upon stepping onto the basement carpet, I found it was completely soaked from the water sprayed into the house from the fire trucks. The basement was the most water damaged room in the house.

I opened a little storage area under the staircase and found a large bin of Dad's prized photographs. I opened the bin to find a lot of them damaged from the water, but there was still a considerable amount that looked like they could be salvaged. I squatted down, looking through the photos. Some of them I had never seen. Dad always took and collected a lot of photos throughout my life. One of the photos I pulled out of the bin and stared at for a while

was a photo taken on my high school graduation day. I was standing in between Mom and Dad, wearing my cap and gown with my arm around Dad
while I held my diploma. The bin was a timeline of photos that pretty much
documented my whole life up until that point. I looked forward to getting
them home and going through them all. There were other keepsakes in the
bin like Dad's discharge papers from the army reserves, a newspaper article
praising him as the quarterback in a high school football game, and a photo
book from Mom and Dad's wedding. Before leaving the house, I went back
to the garage to say another prayer to Dad.

As I walked out of the house, I found Tony waiting in the driveway for
support as he knew that must have been a very difficult situation for me.
Talking about what I had found in the house, I told him I was disappointed
that I wasn't able to find a watch that I had bought for my Dad a few years
back. Tony told me to be sure and looked through everything. He said, "If
you're looking in a drawer with a lot of things, make sure you move things
around because the item could be in an unexpected place." He urged me to
go take another look to be sure the watch wasn't in the house. Something
was telling me that I should go look again.

I went back into the house and upstairs into Dad's bedroom. I opened
the top drawer, which was filled with rolled socks and underwear. Last time
through the house, I wrote off the drawer as just a sock drawer and not a place
where I would likely find the watch. I took Tony's advice and put my hands
in the drawer, moving things around before I heard a metal clank against
the side of the drawer. There was something inside one of the pairs of socks.
I unrolled the socks to find the Gucci watch inside. I couldn't believe I was
actually holding the watch. I ran down the stairs to show Tony, telling him
where I found it and thanked him for encouragement to take a second look.

After spending a few hours at the house, I had seen enough and was ready
to leave. I thanked Tony again for sticking around while I went through the
house. Before leaving the neighborhood, I drove by our old house where we
lived as a family before my parent's divorce in 1981. I sat parked in front of

the house, thinking back to those years in the early '80s. I imagined Dad's first white Cadillac Eldorado parked in the driveway. I thought about the old videos that I still had of my third birthday, a large family gathering for Christmas and a day Dad & I spent rolling skating together in front of the house. As I drove off I thought about when Mom and I left that house when I was five for our move down to Atlanta.

# VALU VENDING

.....................

Leaving Dad's house, I headed over to my estate lawyer's office in Wyandotte. After I arrived, we made our way into the conference room. My most pressing question was his guidance on how I should proceed to keep Dad's vending machine business, Valu Vending, afloat until I could figure out what I was going to do. Dad had built up a great little business over the years, and it generated a lot of cash. I ultimately wanted to sell off the business for what it was worth. Even though Dad always left the door open for me to come back to Detroit to take over his business it wasn't something I was interested in. My life was in California and I didn't want to be in the bar business. My lawyer recommended visiting Dad's customers as soon as I felt comfortable. He suggested that I start to create a contact list along with an inventory list of all of the assets at each account to establish a documented value of the business that could be included as part of the estate. He offered to create a formal letter on behalf of the estate that would be sent out to Dad's customers introducing me as his son who would be taking over operations and requesting their patience while we determine the future of Valu Vending. I knew it was going to require a lot of work as everything at Dad's house and in his van related to Valu Vending was destroyed in the fires. I was going to have to start from scratch in building out the customer and inventory list. My plan was to start asking family and friends of the family about the accounts they knew to be Dad's customers.

As I left my lawyer's office, I called one of Dad's closest friends Jimmy as I knew he would know a lot of Dad's accounts. Jimmy could be obnoxious, which made me a little uncomfortable at times, but he always made me laugh with his Mick Jagger impersonation. He would do this strut, put one hand on his hip, look back, and stick his tongue out, which really did look like Mick Jagger. I questioned a lot of Dad's friends. It was known that Dad had loaned out a lot of money to people over the years, and after he passed away, not one of them came forward to mention any intent of repaying the debt. Dad never put any kind of formal agreements in place either with personal or business loans. Everything was based on a handshake. Jimmy told me that he had a vested interest in Valu Vending as he had invested some of his own money into Dad's business not that long ago. He told me he knew a lot of the accounts. He offered to pick me up in the morning so we could spend the day driving around to as many of the accounts as possible. I thought it would be good to introduce myself in person to Dad's customers while I started to build out the documentation of contacts and inventory.

Jimmy picked me up at Uncle Dave's house in the morning. As I climbed in the back of Jimmy's pickup truck, he introduced me to a guy riding shotgun, Jeff Peterson, who I had never met. Jimmy introduced Jeff as someone who used to work for Dad from time to time when he needed extra help. Considering we didn't have any of the keys to open the vending machines, Jeff was with us to saw the locks off of any that needed servicing. Jeff made me extremely uncomfortable immediately as he had an overwhelming nervous energy to him. Never once during the four to five hours of us driving around did Jeff say anything about Dad or provide any kind of condolences for my loss.

When we met with the bar owners, the usual response was them saying that they were really sorry for my loss; they loved my Dad, and he was the reason why they were a customer of Valu Vending. It started to seem obvious that without Dad in the picture, most of his customers would probably consider partnering with other vending companies moving forward. If the bar owner mentioned anything wrong with the machine, Jeff would saw the lock off so we could access it. The sound of the saw cutting through the lock was extremely loud and a very uncomfortable sound that echoed through the establishment, disturbing the customers. Understanding how the vending business works from helping Dad service accounts in the past, I knew the game and how vending companies were always offering incentives in attempt to take over accounts from their competitors. Since it was a business based on handshakes, there was never any kind of contract in place guaranteeing a partnership for an extended period of time. The bar owners liked to keep their options open. In talking with Jimmy, I found out which bars Dad had loaned money out to for renovations to help attract more people as a hot spot, but again, there wasn't anything in writing. I got a sense that most of the bar owners probably thought with Dad being gone, they were off the hook on the money they owed and there was nothing legally binding.

As we wrapped up the day, I talked with Jimmy about trying to keep things afloat. I wasn't able to be back in Detroit on a full-time basis with my family and career based in California. Jimmy said he would be available to service the accounts in the meantime while I considered potential options for selling off the business. We both had a vested interest to try and sell off Valu Vending for as much as possible. Most of the bar owners knew Jimmy as a friend of Dad's and viewed him as a familiar face, a fact that seemed like it could help keep things business as usual as much as possible. I discussed with Jimmy how we needed to continue to build out the list of accounts and the associated equipment that could be used as part of a potential sale of the business. Anything associated with Valu Vending would be documented as part of Dad's estate, but considering it was a cash-based business with non-active counters on the vending machines, whatever cash was taken from the machines was based on the honor system. I had been through a lot on that trip to Detroit and was ready to go home and be with my family in California.

Uncle Dave drove me to the Detroit airport to catch my flight home. I made my way through security to my gate. I boarded my flight and found my seat against the window. As we took off into the clouds, I kept thinking about that photo I found at Dad's house of my high school graduation, and my mind wandered back to those years.

# FREE BIRD

....................

In September of 1990, Dad was released after completing his sentence of thirty-two months. I imagine those final moments in the facility with him waking up in his cell, filled with excitement knowing it was his last morning in the facility. I imagine Bob Seger's song "Still the Same" playing as the security guard approaches Dad's cell, calling out "Dennis Langley" with Dad already standing there ready to go. The cell door opens and the guard escorts Dad down the corridor amongst all the other inmates still serving time. Dad takes a quick look back at his cell where he spent the past three years of his life. The guard turns him over to security in a front room to begin the check-out process. He completes some paperwork and changes back into his street clothes that he wore when he checked-in which was a black polo shirt, dark jeans, and a pair of white tennis shoes. The staff hands him an envelope of his personal items, which include a gold link bracelet, a gold pinky ring, and a gold rope chain necklace.

Dad walks out of the facility, feeling a strong sense of freedom as he turns around for one final look at the place from the outside before boarding a shuttle to the airport. Dad arrives at the airport, struts through the terminal without any bags, and arrives at his departure gate with the sign displaying Detroit, Michigan. He boards the plane and makes his way to a window seat over the wing. As the plane takes off, he takes in the view while the plane disappears up into the clouds. He lays his head back on the headrest and closes his eyes to get some rest, thinking about what lies ahead. As the plane makes its final descent, he looks out over his hometown. Dad makes his way through airport toward ground transportation. He finds a taxi and jumps in the backseat, providing the driver with his parents' address in Wyandotte. I am looking out the front window of my grandparent's house as Dad's taxi pulls up to the house. I run out the door, giving him a big hug in the driveway. Dad looks me up and down with a big smile on his face. We head into the house with our arms around each other as Dad says "Mom...Dad, I'm home."

After spending some time catching up with my grandparents in the living room, Dad wanted to check out the loft where we would be staying together. I followed him up the stairs into our room as he looked around at our twin beds on opposite sides of the room with a single dresser and small closet. I could tell he was reflecting on the whole scenario of being back at his parent's house at forty-five years old with me, his fourteen-year-old son, looking up to him as we were about to start a whole new chapter in life. He couldn't help but notice my poster of Ice Cube's *AmeriKKKa's Most Wanted* album cover taped to the wall next to my bed. He asked me about it. I told him I was really into rap music and that was my favorite album. Dad was always a fan of music and open to new music trends. Later that night while lying in our beds, Dad told me that we wouldn't be staying there long as he had some things in the works. He said he had some money put away and we should be able to find our own house within a few months. I wasn't worried about anything. I was just happy to be with him.

Dad and I would wake up in the morning together, and after dropping me off at school in Grandpa's car, he would spend the day working on his next business venture. Dad reconnected with Monte, former business partner from his old bar Moby Dick's. Monte was now running his own vending business, servicing bars in the greater Detroit area providing jukeboxes, cigarette machines, pool tables, and video games. Dad started helping Monte with the business to learn how things were run. Monte knew Dad wanted to eventually set up his own business and was ok with it; he told Dad there were plenty of bars in the Detroit area for them both to successfully run their own separate businesses.

Outside of school, I continued to work on improving my basketball skills at Polaski Park. I made the JV team my freshman year, which was highly competitive. Even though I wasn't a starter, Dad was proud as I had only picked up a basketball four months prior. One night after I got home from practice, Dad and Grandpa were hanging out in the living room. Dad asked me how practice went and told me that I could probably get more time in the games if I worked on hustling more and getting faster. I laughed, then joked about how much faster I was than him. Dad said I was dreaming, and even at his age, he would beat me in a running race. We both laughed as Dad said, "Why don't we head out into the street right now and settle this?"

Grandpa, listening to our back-and-forth banter, had a smile ear to ear and followed us out the front door of the house. It was dark with the only light being the streetlights, which were about fifty yards apart. Dad said, "Let's race from one streetlight to the next." Dad and I walked to one of the streetlights, and Grandpa stood where we were to finish. We took our positions, Grandpa calling out, "Ready, set, go!" We started off pretty even, but as the race went on, Dad pulled ahead, winning by a considerable margin. I was out of breath and in disbelief, so I challenged him to another race. We lined up again, and the second race had played out the exact same way. The three of us laughed and joked about the whole scenario as we headed back into the house.

Within a few months, Dad branched off to start up his own vending business that he named Valu Vending. Through his network, he already knew a few bar owners and was able to secure his first couple of customers. He provided customers access to cigarette machines, pool tables, jukeboxes, video games, and dart boards. Valu Vending provided and managed the machines, splitting the profits fifty-fifty with the bar owner. With Valu Vending off the ground, Dad was ready to find us a house. Dad knew a lot of people in Wyandotte and started asking around for anyone looking to sell their home off the market to negotiate a better price. Through word of mouth, he found a guy who was looking to sell a small house about six blocks down the street from Grandma and Grandpa's house. Dad walked over one day, knocked on the door, asked the guy if he would be interested in selling the house and if he could take a look. It was a small one thousand square-foot single-story house with two bedrooms, one bath, and an unfinished basement. It was an outdated old house, but Dad wanted a fixer-upper to modernize it to his taste. Dad liked the potential of the house and made the owner a cash offer, which he accepted. Once he closed on the house, he immediately had my Uncle Chuck start working on some cosmetic upgrades, putting in new floors, countertops, updating the kitchen and bathroom, repainting and expanding the master bedroom. We moved into our new bachelor pad, and I was excited for us to have our own place.

# DAVIS STREET HOUSE

....................

Dad was always in and out of the house, loading up his black work van with cigarettes, parts, and supplies. Focused on expanding the business, he worked long days constantly meeting with bar and restaurants owners within an hour drive from the house. It was a highly competitive industry where it was normal for vendors to offer bar owners cash upfront for them to switch vending service providers. Bar owners always welcomed the incentives that vendors offered to earn their business. It was cut-throat business as the bar owners didn't like signing any kind of long-term agreements, keeping them free to switch vendors at any given time. Vendors had to be sure the machines were always up and running, minimizing downtime as they were a steady stream of revenue for the bar owners. Dad's agreements with the bar owners was always based on a handshake.

One of the ways Dad set himself apart from the other vendors in the beginning was looking for bars that were in a good location but weren't a hot spot for customers. Dad would approach these bar owners, offering to invest into their bar by covering the costs for minor renovations and providing large flat-screen TVs in return for using Valu Vending as their vending service provider. Dad felt if he was able to rejuvenate the bar, it would attract more people, which would generate more cash running through the machines, which would benefit both the bar owner and Valu Vending. Dad looked at it as an investment, and he loved being the driving force behind creating a new hot spot. Dad would cover the initial cost of renovations, working out a deal where the bar owner would get a lower percentage of the profits until the renovation costs were paid off, then everything went to the normal fifty-fifty split. Dad worked hard; all the bar owners liked him right away, and he was enjoying growing his little vending business.

My freshman year consisted of school, basketball, and attending social events. I had become close with a group of guys from school, and we were always together heading out to varsity basketball games, football games, or hanging out at one of our houses together. I became really close with a kid named Jay, who I thought looked like a young Johnny Depp. One day in class, I told him I thought his rasta beaded necklace was cool and we became fast friends who were always together.

That year, Vanilla Ice's "Ice Ice Baby" was the popular song, blasting through car stereos with the bass cranked up, and you heard it everywhere. We loved rap music, and it was reflected in how we dressed. The clothing trends were I.O.U. sweatshirts, Used brand jeans (which were expensive ripped up jeans), Starter coats, and hats with your favorite sports team. I wore a Georgetown Hoyas starter coat and hat because I liked the navy and grey colors. Dad had always appreciated the fashion trends and liked when I bought stuff we could both wear. He didn't understand why my friends and I liked to buy clothing two sizes too big. He got upset one day when I asked for some money to buy a new Ralph Lauren button-down shirt from the mall to wear to a football game and came home with a size XL. When he first saw it folded up in the bag, he got excited and loved the light green color I picked out, but then his expression quickly changed as I took it out of the bag and held it up with him saying, "What size is that? C'mon, that's ridiculous."

Jay was with me, and we laughed as we both started explaining that was the style those days. I told Jay to show Dad his jeans, so he pulled up his oversized sweater to show his baggy Girbaud jeans, which were three sizes too big, barely held up with a belt, and his pink polka-dot boxers showing. Jay and I were having fun with the discussion, telling Dad, "You don't want to be caught out of style wearing a bunch of fitted shit." Dad thought we were ridiculous and walked away from our discussion.

One night, we made plans to meet up with a group of girls from school at a Pizza Hut after the game. Since it was close to my house, the boys and I planned to just walk back to my house afterward. It was a cold night as we strolled down the neighborhood streets, talking about our night. A suspicious-looking car pulled up next to us, and the tinted window on the passenger side rolled down. The song "Mind Playing Tricks on Me" by Geto Boys was playing on the car stereo. It was a group of older guys, and we heard one of them say, "This must be them." They got out of the car and quickly approached us. We were scared as everything was happening so fast; they were older, and it just felt like trouble. One of the guys pulled out a knife, which triggered me and my friends to take off scattering in all different directions to get away. I ran across the street and jumped over a driveway gate into someone's backyard.

Looking over my shoulder, I could see one of the guys trailing behind, so I continued through the yard and hopped over the rear fence into a back alley. I was only about three blocks from my house, so I broke into a sprint down the alley, running as fast as I could. My cardio was strong from basketball, and as I ran, I looked over my shoulder and could see the guy falling farther and farther behind. When I arrived at the house, my friend Rico was already there, and we exchanged stories in between catching our breath as we headed into the house. We were still missing our friend John. We looked out the front window and then saw John running down the street toward my house by himself. With the adrenaline flowing, we compared stories and bragged about how we all got away. None of us knew the guys or why they approached us like that. I think they were just out looking for trouble and wanted to mess with us.

Dad's vending business was growing pretty fast with him constantly acquiring new accounts. He needed my help from time to time, so during the weekends, I would jump in the van while we drove from bar to bar, fixing machines and collecting cash to be split with the bar owners. I really liked driving around with Dad in the work van, listening to music and talking about life. I usually told him about what was going on in school, while playing him my favorite songs. The work van was always a mess with little paper sleeves for coins, machine parts, cartons of cigarettes, CD's, boxes of candy and chips everywhere in the back. It always surprised me when we'd walk into a dark bar early in the morning and find the shades drawn and people hunched over their drinks at the bar like they had been there for hours. Dad told me there were a lot of people who worked night shifts at gas stations and factories, so early morning was their happy hour. One of the mornings, I was caught completely off-guard when a drunk guy got excited to see us come through the front door, shouting, "Dennis!" He came over, asking Dad how he had been and patting him on the back. I became really uncomfortable and tried not to stare when I was introduced because the bridge of his nose looked like it had collapsed or sunken into his face. When leaving the bar that morning, I asked Dad about it, and he said that was George, who was a big partyer back in the day and did way too much cocaine.

# SNOWBOARDING & GRUNGE

. . . . . . . . . . . . . . . . . . . .

Approaching the winter of 1991, I discovered the sport of snowboarding. There was a new show called MTV Sports, which showed ten minute clips of new, emerging alternative sports that had been labeled as "extreme sports." Dan Cortese was the host of the show, and I thought he was so cool with his long hair and how he always wore bandanas. Standing in front of the TV, I watched a clip of Craig Kelly surfing down the snow covered mountain to the intro of the song "There Goes the Neighborhood" by Body Count. I was immediately hooked, thinking the sport was right up my alley with my background in skateboarding. At this point I had taken a few ski trips with Dad to Boyne Mountain in Michigan as a little kid. Skiing had always been a sport Dad really loved. He loved the culture and clothing of the sport. He even had the classic '80s Lange ski girl posters framed on the walls at his previous house in Farmington Hills. Prior to his time in Minnesota, he took regular trips to Aspen in the winter and never missed Crazy Days, which was a big party for St. Patrick's Day at Boyne Mountain in Michigan.

For Christmas that year, I asked Dad about getting a snowboard and all the gear to give it a try. Dad took me to a cool little ski shop over the holidays. Walking in felt similar to that day we went into the skate shop in Newport Beach when I got my first skateboard. I loved seeing all of the boards and outdoor clothing designed to keep you warm and dry out on the mountain. The clothing reminded me very much of skateboarding apparel, only it was made for the snow. I picked out a Kemper Cyclone board and a complete Burton outfit. Now that I was ready to ride, Dad and I took a few day trips together over the holidays to Alpine Valley and Pine Knob, which were small resorts about an hour away from the house. Dad thought it was cool that I was getting into a new trend with snowboarding and enjoyed watching me learn a different way to get down the mountain from skiing. At the time, there weren't many people on the hill snowboarding, so it almost felt like the early days of skateboarding all over again.

Eager to improve, I was always looking for a way to get to the slopes. My friend Jay, who also used to skateboard before we met, had gotten a snowboard over the holidays. There was a small ski run at the local golf course next to our school that ran a single chairlift up the hill in the winter. The hill was a landfill, so it got the nickname of Mount Trashmore. Jay was sixteen, and he had his driver's license and an old beat-up brown Ford Escort that he named "DooDoo Brown", so he was able to drive us to the resort. Mount Trashmore had night skiing with lights that lit up the hill. Jay picked me up on a Friday night, and we spent the whole evening out on the hill, having a blast snowboarding in the blistering cold. There was a little jump right under the chairlift where we spent hours watching each other trying to do old skateboard tricks off the jump.

Later that evening, I lost track of Jay and realized I hadn't seen him on the hill for a while. I headed into the lodge, looking for him, but he was nowhere to be found. After spending some time in the lodge warming up, I headed back out, thinking maybe I missed him in the lodge and he was back on the mountain. I was starting to worry when I saw him strolling back to the hill from the parking lot with his board under his arm and a big smile on his face. I went over to him to figure out where he had been. Jay said he met a girl in the lodge, and they had sex out in his car. I didn't believe him at first, but Jay was a pretty good-looking kid, and he had a way with the girls. As it approached midnight, the resort was about to close, so it was time to head home. We strolled back to the car, talking about how much fun we had snowboarding that night.

As spring approached, Dad started talking about *Crazy Days* at Boyne Mountain for St. Patrick's Day and was excited for me to experience his favorite weekend. I was only a few months away from turning sixteen and couldn't wait to be able to drive. Dad would offer to let me drive the car home from church on Sundays if I would attend with him. He had always been pretty regular attending church, but never forced me to go as he wanted me to choose to go on my own. Considering the incentive to drive the car home, I was in church every Sunday and enjoyed driving home through the dirty slushy roads in Wyandotte.

I became attracted to a new era in rock music, which was being called "grunge rock". A switch flipped in me the first time I heard Nirvana's "Smells Like Teen Spirit." I was instantly hooked on that new sound. It pulled me away from hip-hop and grunge started to become all I wanted to listen to. Pearl Jam had put out the music video for their first single, "Alive" and I picked up their first album *Ten*. It was the beginning of a change in my style, and I wanted to grow my hair out from the short clean cut look I had for years. I wanted to look like one of the surfers from *Point Break* which became my favorite movie during this time. I loved Nirvana's *Nevermind*, so when I saw a poster of the album cover at the music store, I had to have it and taped it up on my bedroom wall.

It was time for my first Crazy Days at Boyne Mountain for St. Patrick's Day weekend. Dad and I loaded up our ski and snowboard gear into Dad's work van, putting it on top of all the boxes of cigarettes and vending machine products in the back. Dad rented a cabin, and few others from our family were planning to be up at Boyne as well. The weather looked perfect with clear skies and warmer temperatures. On the drive up, I played Nirvana's *Nevermind* and a new tape I had picked up, which was Soundgarden's *Badmotorfinger*. Dad asked me about my change in music and the Nirvana poster up in my room. I told him I thought this new wave of music called grunge rock was cool. We arrived in Boyne the night before the big party and checked into our cabin to get some rest. Dad was up early in the morning, excited for the day. He wanted to get to the mountain early to beat the traffic. We got ready and hopped back into the work van to head to the mountain. It was a beautiful morning with the sun rising in clear blue skies.

As we approached the resort, it was clear to me that it was going to be a big day as the parking lot was already filled with people getting ready for the party on the mountain. The parking lot had a fun vibe with people in ski hats that looked like they had different color dread locks and some wearing retro onesie ski suits. Once we had our lift tickets, we headed into the lodge as Dad wanted to grab a Bloody Mary to kick off the day. Walking to the lift, I asked about what looked to be a big pool carved into the snow at the base of the mountain in front of the lodge. Dad explained it was for the slush cup event at the end of the day, which was a contest to see who could ski down the mountain and basically water-ski across the water, making it to the other side.

We made our way through the lift lines for our first run. On the lift ride up, I got excited as I spotted a little snowboard terrain park a few runs over and told Dad I had to go check it out. On the lift, Dad pointed out this little house, which he called the warming hut, just down from the top of the main run, called Victor. He said, "that is where the party will be all day." Dad knew I wanted to head to the terrain park, so he told me to meet him back at the warming hut for lunch. I spent the whole morning in the terrain park trying to pull off some of my old skateboard tricks. Dad alternated between taking a few runs then hitting the bar in the lodge at the bottom of the mountain, which was packed with people having a great time. We met at the warming hut just before lunch, and they were getting ready for the party, setting up speakers and an outdoor bar. We took a quick run together to the bottom to grab a couple of hamburgers they were grilling outside on the deck.

After lunch, we headed back up to the warming hut halfway up the mountain with the party in full swing. The music was loud, and everyone was spread out across the mountain with their beers and cocktails. I loved seeing everyone having a great time on the mountain closing down the season until next year. Mid-afternoon, the slush cup event was announced over the loudspeaker, so we headed down to join the crowd around the edges of the pool carved into the snow. One after the other, people skied or snowboarded down the hill in various costumes and goofy outfits as the announcer called their names over the loudspeaker. With each contestant, the crowd either let out a loud "aww" if they crashed into the water or cheered loudly if they made it across. The weather was perfect, and the spring weather was refreshing after the long winter. We headed back to the cabin before the slush cup was over to avoid the crowds and stopped by a grocery store to pick up some food to cook on the grill for dinner. We hung out at the cabin and talked about how much fun we had that day. The next morning, we packed up the work van and headed home.

# SOUTHBOUND

·····················

As the summer approached that year, I became attracted to the idea of moving back down to Atlanta for my last two years of high school. I had originally moved up to Detroit to be there for Dad after his time in Minnesota, but I liked living in the South. I missed the greenery with all of the trees, the heavy rain storms, mild winters and the laid back culture. Dad seemed to be on a good path, building up his vending business, and was on the road most of the time. One weekend while helping Dad service the route, I brought up my thoughts to him about potentially moving back down to Atlanta. I explained to him how I felt like I fit in better down in Georgia. He was completely open to the idea, saying he wanted me to do whatever made me happy. He said I was always welcome to come stay with him whenever I wanted or could move back any time. I told him I was going to bring it up to Mom and see how she felt about it. Dad told me he was planning to buy me a car before the summer, but it probably made more sense to figure things out after the move back down to Georgia.

I called Mom later that evening to tell her my thoughts. She was ecstatic about the idea of me coming back down to live with her and Peter for my last two years of high school. I felt relieved that both Mom and Dad were on board and I started to get excited about the move. I knew I would be going to a completely new school while I lived with Mom and Peter in Buckhead, and I looked forward to reinventing myself with a fresh start at a new school. It was settled, and things were in motion that once I finished my sophomore year, I would be heading back down South to get situated before starting my junior year.

As the school year came to an end, I asked Dad if I could have a going-away party at the house with my friends. Dad mentioned a Friday where he planned to be on the road most of the evening visiting accounts, so I invited my friends over. I asked Dad if they all could stay the night. Dad knew we were probably approaching that age where we could be drinking, so he felt letting everyone stay at the house was a good idea. My usual group of friends stopped by for one last get-together at the house as a farewell before my move to Georgia. Jay was the life of the party, bringing over some beer and a hip-hop mix tape. At first, we were all nervous about the beers as we were new to drinking. It was just us at the house as we cracked open the big forty-ounce bottles of beer, popped in Jay's hip-hop tape and cranked up Dad's house stereo. We talked about our memories together over the past few years. They couldn't believe I was moving to Georgia. I told them they had to come visit me as the South was a lot of fun.

A few hours later, Jay pulled me aside, showing me couple of "joints" in his hand which just looked like homemade cigarettes. I knew what they were growing up around marijuana. He said, "Let's break away and go smoke one behind the garage in the alley." It seemed exciting and I was curious what it was like so I followed him out the side door into the sunshine as we walked by Dad's old red '70s Bronco that had been parked in the driveway the past year. Dad acquired the Bronco through a deal with one of his customers and planned to restore it but hadn't gotten around to it yet. We walked through the little walkway between the side of the garage and a fence that was used to take the trash into the alley for pickup.

I could still hear the hip-hop music playing from the house with the side door open as Jay lit up the joint and passed it over to me after taking the first hit. I took a hit, coughed out some smoke and we joked about if we were even doing it right. We talked about how close of friends we had become, and I told him he should come stay with me sometime over the next couple of summers. As the sun started to set, we were all pretty drunk. Dad pulled into the driveway, and we got nervous. I turned down the music, and we sat on the couch like we had just been watching TV as Dad walked into the house. He knew immediately what had been going on. I followed him into his room and came clean that we had been drinking. He made sure everyone was planning to stay the night, which I confirmed. He told me we needed to wind down the party. Later that night, while the rest of us were sleeping out in the living room, Jay and my friend Steve, who were staying in my bedroom while I took the couch, quietly made a drunken video with my camcorder, saying their goodbyes and how much they were going to miss me when I moved to Georgia which I still have.

# BUCKHEAD HOUSE

......................

Beginning of summer in 1992, I flew down to Atlanta with only a suitcase of clothes to start a new chapter in my life. Mom & Peter had moved from the townhouse, where Peter lived when they met, into a sprawling 9,000 sq ft house on a private pond off of West Conway Drive in Buckhead. The Buckhead house has always been my favorite of any house and a place that became to feel like home. The house looked like a large modern white stucco castle. It was hidden from the main road, down a long steep winding driveway, surrounded with large dense trees. My room was in the back of the house on ground level and had French doors that opened up to a garden on one side and also had direct access to the two-story terrace with the pool. There was a small rock waterfall that flowed from the upper level of the terrace down to the charcoal stone pool on the bottom level of the terrace. I loved leaving my door open to hear the sound of water flowing down the waterfall. The house was filled with Peter's modern art collection which I came to really appreciate over the years. Peter had a painting by Jean-Michel Basquiat that became one of my favorite pieces. My favorite artist became Todd Murphy, who was a local artist, that had a very dark style painting on plexiglass over photographs giving the image more dimension than a regular painting. Peter bought one of his first major pieces and he became a friend of the family. There were many photographs throughout the house of celebrities and musicians. Later down the road Mom & Peter gifted me a 1969 black & white photograph of Robert Plant from Led Zeppelin, which I still have as a prized possession. The Buckhead house was designed for entertaining and we had many unforgettable parties at that house over the years.

Shortly after getting situated in the Buckhead house from my move, Mom & Peter sat me down to talk about schools. Peter told me ultimately it would be up to me if I wanted to attend the local public school, but strongly encouraged me to go to a private school. Mom had set appointments for the two of us to visit three or four local private schools in the area. I connected most with St. Pius, which was a Catholic high school, very similar to my previous school in Michigan. We applied and I was accepted to start my junior year in the fall.

St. Pius was about a thirty-minute drive from the house so I needed a car. Mom & Peter took me car shopping at a handful of local dealerships. It was fun driving around with them and looking at all of the options for my first car. We came across a used black Toyota Celica with a manual transmission and I was drawn to it because it seemed like a little sports car to me. Peter really liked the car, worked out the best deal possible and paid cash for the car. That car became my access to freedom, which started a trend of me spending many evenings over in Marietta where I grew up meeting up with friends.

I started to become close with a group of friends who liked to drink, smoke weed and were experimenting with psychedelics. Drinking was still a new thing for me and I was completely against it my first two years of high school, but my group of friends all seem to come from good families, lived in nice neighborhoods, so I felt like I was in good company. We usually were looking for someone whose parents were out of town so we had a place to hang out. I was very cautious about drinking and driving, so if we were going to be partying, I always asked to stay the night out. Peter didn't understand why I always wanted to stay out, telling me I was too old for sleepovers. I would explain how I didn't want to drive thirty minutes home at the end of the night when I was tired, and he usually just let me go. Once I got the green light, I was excited to see where the night would take me and free to have as much fun as possible as long as I was home early in the morning.

Toward the end of the summer, Peter's company, Horizon Carpets, was bought by one of the industry giants, Mohawk Carpets. Considering Peter was the CEO of Horizon Carpets, he made out extremely well from the acquisition. Mom & Peter started to travel more with Peter showing Mom parts of the world she had never seen. While traveling, they always had one of their friends either stay at the house or check on me while they were gone. It was a fun summer, hanging out by our pool during the day and hunting for house parties at night. I started throwing parties at the Buckhead house while Mom & Peter were traveling and had some pretty wild nights. I always tried to keep everyone outside on the two-story terrace so I could just hose it down to clean the next day. The house had an outdoor speaker system and was secluded enough that I didn't need to worry about the neighbors calling the police for being too loud. Like Dad, I liked hosting parties and seeing everyone having a good time.

I showed up for my first day at St. Pius excited to be a new kid on the block. Walking the halls, I got the sense that most of the kids had grown up in the same school system together as it seemed like a lot of them had known each other for years. I didn't feel pressure to make friends right away because I had a good group of friends in Marietta that I had started hanging out with over the summer.

Shortly after I started school that year, Mom and Peter had a trip planned to spend a few weeks in Europe. One of my mom's younger friends, Paula, was going to be staying at the house while they were gone. I knew there was a Friday night where Paula wouldn't be at the house, so I used it as a way to break the ice with the kids at my school, walking the halls and inviting some of them to a party at my house after school. About seven or eight kids showed up and I had a great time getting to know them over beers by the pool. A few days after the party, I heard someone had asked if I was a nark trying to figure out who the partyers were at the school which I thought was funny and never denied it.

# LOLLAPALOOZA 92

. . . . . . . . . . . . . . . . . . .

One morning at school, I was called down to the office over the intercom. Not sure what was going on, I showed up to the front office with one of the admins telling me that my house keeper Paula had called. She had forgotten about a dentist appointment I had that day. The situation seemed strange to me, but I went with it as I got to leave early. I arrived back at the house, Paula's car wasn't there but a buddy's car was parked in the driveway.

As I walked into the kitchen, I saw two of my buddies outside on the back patio, laughing and joking with each other. I walked out onto the patio, confused, and asked why they were at the house. They told me how they had skipped school and drove over to see if Paula would check me out because they had an extra ticket to the music festival Lollapalooza. That year, the lineup included Pearl Jam, Soundgarden, Red Hot Chili Peppers, Rage Against the Machine, Ice Cube, Cypress Hill, Temple of the Dog, Ministry, Porno for Pyros, Tool, and Stone Temple Pilots. The show was at Lakewood Amphitheater, which was a large outdoor venue. We had general admission tickets, which were first come, first served for a spot on the large grass section behind the assigned seats. The concert was an all-day event, and I offered to drive since they had picked up my ticket.

On the way to the venue, my buddies told me they had some mushrooms to take before the show. We each ate a couple once we arrived at the parking lot. We made our way into the venue and found a great spot center stage on the grassy hill under the sun. I couldn't believe a single concert included so many of the artists that I loved. The mushrooms started to take effect during the Chili Peppers' performance as someone handed me this device that looked like one of those old View-Master toys with a mouthpiece attached. You would look through the viewer, and when you blew through the mouthpiece, these mini fans would spin over your eyes, changing the colors of whatever you were looking at. I laid on my back, looking up at the clear blue sky, enjoying the visuals from the device which made the sky multi-colored listening to the Chili Peppers live. For Pearl Jam and Soundgarden, I knew all of their songs and was completely fixated on their performances. I loved seeing Ice Cube, one of my favorite rap artists, and thought it was cool how the show had a blend of rap and alternative rock.

As day turned to night, Ministry took the stage. Their sound was unlike anything else I had heard before. They took hard rock to a whole other level. A bright strobe light flickered over the audience during their performance of "N.W.O." as a large pit of people crashed around in a circle, throwing things up in the air and creating what looked like a mini tornado in front of the stage. We had spent about ten hours at the show that day, and by the end, the effects of the mushrooms had diminished, so we headed back to the house, exchanging story's about our experience and favorite performances.

# MIDNIGHT WRANGLER

..................

Over the course of the school year, I started to really like Jeep Wranglers. I loved the ruggedness of them and saw them as the ultimate go anywhere adventure vehicle. I started to get into the outdoor lifestyle, always looking for an opportunity to go camping in the North Georgia mountains, meet up with friends at the river, or go wakeboarding on the lake. I asked Mom & Peter about the possibility of trading in my Toyota Celica for a Jeep. Peter made me a deal that if I kept my GPA above a 3.5 average, they would get me a Jeep at the end of the school year. As my birthday approached in April and with only a few months left in the school year, we started looking at Jeeps.

One day, we were driving back to the house, and I saw this midnight-blue Jeep suspended up in the air by a crane over the parking lot of a local dealership. I asked Mom if we could go take a look at it. As the salesman approached us in the parking lot, I pointed up at the Jeep and asked if we could take a look at it. The salesman lowered the Jeep down to the ground. As I walked around the outside, I fell in love with it. I loved the dark blue metallic color, light gray vinyl interior, bigger off-road tires, aftermarket aluminum wheels, side step bars, and steel bumpers. Mom could tell this was my favorite Jeep out of the ones we had looked at, but it was more expensive than the base model Jeeps we had been looking at. Mom told me that it was more than they were looking to spend and we would find another one so we'll keep looking. I was disappointed because it was perfect and feared it would be sold in no time.

A few days later on the morning of my seventeenth birthday, I woke up to someone ringing the doorbell early in the morning. I assumed Mom or Peter would go to the door, but it rang again shortly after. I headed to the front door, wondering what was going on. Mom & Peter were nowhere to be found. I opened the large front door to see the blue Jeep parked in the driveway with a large bow on the hood. I could hardly contain my excitement as I walked around with Peter taking pictures of the moment. It turned out Mom knew it was the right Jeep, so when we got home from the dealership, she immediately took Peter back over there to see it, and he loved it. I couldn't wait to drive it to school. I headed back into the house and quickly got ready for school. Before leaving, I put the soft top down and removed the top half of the doors. I felt rugged driving a manual transmission Jeep. I loved feeling the wind blow through the cabin and having a complete open view of the sky while blasting my music. I couldn't wait to pull into the school parking lot that day and show it to my friends.

As the school year came to an end, I made plans to take a road trip up to Detroit to spend a few weeks with Dad to start the summer break. I was looking forward to taking my Jeep on a long road trip and show it to Dad. Before I left town, I picked up a wooden dugout and a one hitter to smoke out of on my trip. It was a beautiful morning the day I was leaving so I sat on the back patio outside my room and took a couple of puffs just after sunrise. I walked out to the Jeep, threw my duffle bag on the backseat and put my large envelope of CDs on the passenger seat. I took the soft top down and pulled the top half of the doors off putting them in the back. I hit the road heading north on I-75. I loved the landscape driving through North Georgia, Tennessee and Kentucky seeing all of the lush green trees and rolling hills. Allman Brother's *Live at Fillmore East* fit that trip perfectly and that album still always reminds me of that road trip. I reached Toledo midafternoon and got excited as I knew I was getting close to Dad's house.

As I drove into Wyandotte, I loved seeing some of the familiar roads and places from when I lived with Dad at the Davis Street House. I arrived around dinnertime, and as I pulled into the driveway, Dad came out, happy to see me and check out the Jeep. I parked behind his new white early '90s Cadillac Eldorado. It was a modern version of the same one he had when I was a little kid. After showing him the Jeep, I asked about the new Cadillac, which he was proud to show off. He told me that he only drove it on special occasions as it wasn't a good car for work. Over the next few weeks, we spent our time together, visiting with family for barbeques at Uncle Dave's backyard pool, or relaxing at Dad's house while he cooked on the grill. It was fun to be back in the house where I use to live with Dad. My bedroom was still set up the same as it had been before I moved to Georgia. It had only been a little over a year since my move to Georgia, but it felt like so much had changed. Dad still had my Haro Freestyle bike in the basement, so I would ride it with Dad on his Rollerblades around the neighborhood streets. He enjoyed Rollerblading as it was like speed skating to him, only he could skate on the streets during the summer. He had this flexible device that was a speaker that he hung around his neck. He liked to skate around the neighborhood for exercise, listening to music. Looking back it is very similar to how I love to ride my bike or ski/snowboard listening to music.

While in town I helped Dad on the vending route, usually during collection days. As we drove around from bar to bar, it was impressive how much Dad had grown his business over the past year with all of his new accounts. He seemed happy and content with everything going on in his life. I told him all about my past year living in Georgia with Mom & Peter. Just like in previous years I played him my favorite music while we drove around which was Smashing Pumpkins album *Siamese Dream*. Dad liked to keep up with the latest music trends and told me he was going to put the album in his CD jukeboxes for customers. After a few weeks, it was time for me to head back down south. I gave Dad a big hug, and we said our goodbyes until the Christmas holidays in the winter. I loaded my stuff into the Jeep and hit the road on I-75 South back down to Georgia.

# MOUNTAIN BIKING

......................

In the beginning of my senior year I fell in love with the sport of mountain biking. I had found out about a local trail system by the Chattahoochee River called Sope Creek, and I wanted to start riding the trails. I viewed mountain biking as a modern version of BMX, only riding on mountain trails instead of a track. Just like with skateboarding and snowboarding, I felt like I was getting into a new, up-and-coming sport. I started my research, visiting local bike shops whenever I could to talk with the shop owners learning about the different bikes. That fall, I got my first mountain bike, which was a 1993 Trek 930 Singletrack. I was drawn to the two-tone purple-and-green frame of the bike.

I became obsessed with the sport, always looking to go ride the Sope Creek trails whenever I could after school or on the weekends. I was happiest driving to the trails with my bike on the back of the Jeep with the top down on a sunny day blasting Smashing Pumpkins *Siamese Dream or* Soundgarden's *Superunknown.* For Christmas that year, Mom and Peter bought me a book of the trails located in the North Georgia mountains. One Saturday afternoon, I took a road trip up to North Georgia to go ride one of the trails I had picked out of the book. Back then, there were no car GPS systems or smartphones, so you had to figure everything out at the house before heading to the trails. The trail was hard to find, and I got lost on the drive. I pulled into a gas station to ask for directions, but the guy behind the counter had no idea what I was talking about regarding trails to ride my mountain bike. After some trial and error, I ended up finding the trailhead. It was such a rush being out on the trails with no one in sight, the smell of the clean mountain air, and the ability to ride anywhere on a bike designed for rugged terrain.

# WESTBOUND

....................

Toward the end of 1993, Mom & Peter asked me my thoughts on where I wanted to go to college. Initially, I was pretty focused on attending University of Georgia. Peter encouraged me to consider going someplace completely new outside of Georgia to get out of my comfort zone and have a completely unique experience. Peter told me attending UGA would probably be a very similar scenario as high school; I'd stay in Georgia and probably continue to hang out with a lot of the same friends. Peter opened my mind up to consider broader options and asked me, "If you could go anywhere, is there anything that comes to mind?"

I immediately thought about Colorado, thinking it would be fun to go mountain biking and snowboarding in the Rockies. Mom & Peter loved the idea and told me to consider applying to mountain town colleges in Colorado. When I brought up the discussion with Dad, he was so happy to hear I was focused on college. Dad loved the idea of me heading to Colorado, telling me how much he loved skiing out there in the winter. He told me the Rockies made Boyne Mountain look like a hill in someone's backyard.

College was becoming a big topic of conversation at school among the seniors. One of my friends had a brochure for Colorado State University in class one day and I asked if I could check it out. As I looked through the brochure, I loved seeing the photos of campus with the mountains in the background. I ended up applying to University of Georgia, Appalachian State, and Colorado State University, which was my top choice. I was excited at the idea of venturing across the country for a completely new experience in Colorado. I was accepted into all three colleges, and it was decided I would be heading off to Colorado State in the fall.

# A DAY TO REMEMBER

·····················

For one of my final assignments my senior year, I wrote a paper about my favorite artist, Todd Murphy, who lived in an old mattress factory, in downtown Atlanta. Todd had become close with Mom & Peter over the years as they purchased one of his first big pieces. For Christmas earlier that year, Todd made a painting just for me and brought it over to the house as a gift. For my paper, I scheduled a time for Todd to provide a tour of his studio and learn about the inspirations behind his work. It was a fun experience getting a glimpse into the mind of an artist dedicated to his work. I thought it was so cool he lived in an old big open warehouse. After the tour, we climbed up the fire escape onto the roof of the building with a view of the downtown Atlanta city lights. He asked me about college and I told him how excited I was to ride my mountain bike out west. He told me when he was younger he rode a bike from New York to Atlanta. It was overwhelming to think of someone riding that long of a distance, but thought it was one of the coolest things I had ever heard. He told me that if I had any interest to ride from Atlanta out to Colorado, he would follow me in my Jeep, to watch me do it, and we could camp out along the way. At the time it seemed like such a far-fetched idea but looking back that would have been such a cool life experience.

Dad flew down with Aunt Cathy to stay with us for my high school graduation ceremony and party at the house. I loved looking up into the crowd and seeing Dad & Aunt Cathy sitting with Mom & Peter. After the ceremony, Aunt Cathy took a photo of me standing in between Mom & Dad. I had one arm around Dad's shoulder showing my diploma. It's my favorite photo that I have with Mom & Dad. It's the one I found in Dad's bin of photos, going through his house after the crime, that brought me back to my high school years. I remember how proud Dad was of me that day. I can still hear his voice telling me "You'll always remember this day Brett".

Shortly after the graduation ceremony Mom & Peter let me invite my friends over for a celebration at the house. We all tried not to schedule our graduation party on the same day as other friends so we could all round robin to everyone's party without the conflict of deciding which one to go to. I had a big group of friends stop by early afternoon to hang out by the pool with everyone planning to stay the night. I loved introducing Dad to my high school friends in Atlanta. Peter took a photo of all of us from the 2$^{nd}$ story terrace looking down on everyone gathered together around the pool raising their drinks in celebration that we had blown up to a poster sized print. My parents were around hanging out with everyone in the afternoon but as the night went on they gave us our space and let loose. We had a great time talking about our high school memories and where everyone was heading off to college in the fall.

# SLOPESIDE MEMORIAL BIRTHDAY

....................

As the captain came over the speaker system announcing our final descent into Orange County, it brought me back to 2008, returning from my trip to go through Dad's house after the crime. I walked out of the sliding glass doors of the airport to find Jenn & Jake waiting for me in Jenn's white SUV by the curb. On the way back to the house, I told Jenn about my experience going through Dad's house. I showed her the Gucci watch that she was familiar with and told her the story behind how I found it. I mentioned Dad's bin of photos that I had shipped to the house and how much I was looking forward to going through them.

That Sunday March 23rd, 2008 would have been Dad's Sixty-third Birthday and he had only passed away just three weeks earlier. Easter fell on the same day that year which seemed like such a crazy coincidence. I decided to spend the day snowboarding at our local Big Bear resort as it always made me feel close to him since it was our favorite thing to do together. I woke up early in the morning, loaded my gear into the trunk, and secured my board in the roof rack on my Audi. It was just before sunrise as I got on the road, heading East toward the mountains.

When I arrived in Big Bear early morning the sun was shining down on the snow covered mountain with clear blue skies. I got ready to ride for the day amongst everyone else in the parking lot and felt similar to getting ready with Dad for Crazy Days in Michigan. I laced up my snowboard boots, put on a light weight spring ski shell, put my goggles on my head before locking up the car and heading toward the mountain with my board under my arm. I stopped by the ticket office to get a day pass and continued toward the lift. I had a strong sense that Dad was right there with me that day and I wanted to show him my local mountain. I usually called him on my way home from these trips to tell him about my day, and we had talked about plans for him to join me at Big Bear someday.

I hopped on the lift to break in my legs for the first run of the day. As I carved down the run, I felt Dad's presence right there alongside me, skiing down the mountain. It was such a beautiful day with perfect spring conditions. I spent the whole morning running laps down the mountain snowboarding while I had Pearl Jam's *The Long Road* playing on repeat in my headphones as it fit my mood that day.

As lunch approached, I made my way to the outdoor patio at the base of the mountain, which was packed with people congregated around the bar area mingling with their drinks. The sun had warmed up the base of the mountain by now with everyone stripped down into t-shirts, enjoying the warm sunshine and the music playing through the outdoor speaker system. As I grabbed a beer from the bar, I got emotional thinking about how Dad had only passed away just three weeks before his Birthday, what had happened to him and the reality of him being gone. I thought about all of our ski trips together over the years and how much we both loved being out on the mountain. I thought about my conversation with my Mom and my initial thoughts of wanting to put Dad's ashes in the back bowls of Vail, Colorado. I thought about how spreading his ashes at ski resorts would be the perfect way to honor his legacy. It would also be a way to bond with Jake in the future revisiting the locations once he was old enough to ski with me. I felt strong about the decision and was convinced that after keeping Dad's ashes with us at the house for a while I would start spreading them at places where we had skied together or resorts where Dad would have loved to ski. I was getting visibly emotional thinking about it so I pulled my goggles down to cover my watery eyes and headed back to the lifts to spend a few more hours out on the mountain before heading home. The drive home late afternoon felt strange not being able to call Dad to hear his voice and talk with him about my day snowboarding.

# DAD'S PHOTOGRAPHS

....................

It was early April 2008, just before my thirty-second Birthday, when Dad's bin of photos arrived at the house. It was a sunny Saturday morning, I took the bin upstairs into my home office, sat on the floor and unlatched the top of the large storage container. It had a uncomfortably strong smell of smoke from the fire at the house. I started to go through them pulling out the large clumps of photos that had bonded together from getting wet then drying. Some of the clumps were unsalvageable and unfortunately I had to just throw them away. There were photos I had never seen, dating back to the years before I was born. There were some where I had seen the photo in the past, but then there were multiple versions where Dad had taken many photos of the same point in time.

As I peeled apart one of the clumps, I came across a photo of Dad that I had never seen before. It was a profile shot of him driving his boat *Magic* in the early '80s with his longer hair wind-blown back. It looked like a perfect day out on the lake with sun rays reflecting off his sunglasses. He looked happy and completely content in the photo. The photo became slightly damaged when I broke it apart from a clump of photos it created a line across the middle of the photo from the other photo it was bonded to but I thought it created a cool element to the vintage photo. It has become my favorite photo of my dad and how I like to remember him.

As I continued to go through the photos it was like looking through a timeline of my past. Some of the recent photos of Dad I had never seen since there was a gap of about 8 years leading up to the crime where I hadn't taken any trips back to Detroit as he came to visit me. Looking through the photos of my younger years made me think how everything had shaped my life into the man I had become as a father and how I was looking forward to experiencing the same milestones in life with Jake in the coming years. I thought about how my life could have been completely different if I hadn't gone off to college in Colorado where I met my wife Jennifer. I thought about how my life intertwined with Dad's over the years when we would get together usually during the Holidays. I thought about how much he supported me over the years allowing me to roam freely figuring out my own path in life.

One of the photos I came across was a photo of me sitting on a ledge outside of a room I rented at a house in Hollywood, California after graduating from college in 1998. I have a cordless phone next to me that I used to make calls looking for work as I chased my dreams in the film industry. My friend Jay took the photo while visiting me before he moved to the area a year later. I wasn't sure how Dad had the photo but staring at it took me back to those years in my life, when I left the nest, venturing out on my own to start college.

# OFF HE GOES

....................

During the summer of 1994, I worked full time at Peter's new rug & home accessory story called Horizon Pacific, to save up as much money as possible for college in the fall. As it got close to the time to head off to Colorado State, Mom wanted to take me clothes shopping at Phipps Plaza, which was a high-end mall close to the house in Buckhead. As we walked around, I was focused on jeans, sweaters, flannels, lace-up boots, beanies and jackets for the winter. One of the department stores had a Ralph Lauren section called Double RL, which was their high-quality ranch-inspired clothing, and was exactly what I was looking for. I found a thick wool cream-and-black houndstooth button-up with brown suede elbow patches and a khaki field jacket that I loved. The clothes were expensive, so Mom told me that she would buy the shirt and jacket, but I wouldn't be able to get much else. I agreed with Mom, that it was better to have a few nice quality pieces of clothing rather than more cheaper clothes. I imagined myself getting out of the Jeep in Colorado looking like I lived on a mountain ranch. I had a great time shopping with Mom and spending time with her over lunch talking about our final days together before heading off to college.

The day had come to hit the road. Garrett, one of my close friends, was going to join me for the drive and then fly back to Georgia. I had used some of my graduation money to buy an aftermarket hardtop for the Jeep, which would be much better in the Colorado winters. I packed the Jeep with my stereo, a TV/VCR combo, clothes, mountain bike on the spare tire rack, and my snowboard on the roof rack. As we sat in the Jeep ready to go, Mom was barely holding back tears. She had thought of something at the last minute and asked us to hold on while she ran into the house. She came back out with a bottle of Maker's Mark and handed it to Garrett in the passenger seat. She said, "Here is something to celebrate with once you make it Colorado." We drove up the long driveway, and I looked in the rearview mirror to see my mom waving us off as she faded into the distance.

After a full day of driving, we almost ran out of gas near east St. Louis in a rough part of town. We barely made it to a gas station, and it was dark with no one around except one other guy filling up his old Cadillac. I tried to make small talk, asking if the station was open as there was no one there. The guy didn't respond and just stared at me. I started to get worried because you could see everything I owned through the back windows of the Jeep. I walked over to the window where you would normally pay for the gas, but there was no one there. I knocked on the window, and a disheveled lady came out from the back. She seemed annoyed.

When I asked to pay for gas, she said, "I suggest you fill up quick and get out of here. There aren't a whole lot of white boys coming around here."

Once the Jeep was full, we got back on the highway as quick as possible and felt relieved to be on our way again. We took turns driving throughout the night but the Jeep was hard to sleep in as the seats didn't recline. From St. Louis, it was a straight shot on I-70 to Denver. As the sun came up the next morning, we cheered crossing the Colorado state line. Driving on I-70 by the ski resorts of Vail, Breckenridge, through the Eisenhower tunnel, and then Loveland Pass was the prettiest stretch of highway I had ever seen. I couldn't believe this was going to be my new home for the foreseeable future. We finally made it to Fort Collins in the afternoon and drove around looking for a hotel to check into. This was the first time I had seen the town & campus. We found an older Spanish-style hotel down the street from the main campus near what was called Old Town. That night, we cracked open the bottle of Maker's Mark and celebrated in our hotel room.

The next morning, I woke up early extremely hungover but could hardly contain my excitement to check out the campus. While Garrett was still asleep, I grabbed my mountain bike and rode to campus. I rode up to the

Oval, which was a focal point on campus. It was a large circular drive with buildings all around, and then through the center of the oval was a sidewalk lined with large trees and grass on both sides. I stood in the middle of the Oval, taking in how beautiful that part of the campus was, and couldn't believe this was my new school. I rode over to the student center, which had a little pond out front and a view of the local Horsetooth Mountains and Reservoir. I rode by my dorm, Parmalee Hall, which I would be moving into in just a few days. Parmalee was close to the student center and a short walk to my classes on campus.

When I got back to the hotel, I was overwhelmed with excitement telling Garrett how awesome the campus was, urging him to come check it out. We jumped in the Jeep, I drove him through campus and then we headed up into Horsetooth to check out the large reservoir in the local mountains. Over the next few days we explored the whole area so I could get familiar with the town until I was able to move into my dorm.

Move-in day was here, and I started unloading all of my belongings from the Jeep into my new dorm room. It was exciting to see all of my other dorm mates for the school year moving into their rooms. Parmalee was one of the nicest dorms on campus being the newest development. The rooms had Jack and Jill bathrooms instead of a community bathroom like most of the other dorms. My new roommate walked in, whose name was Matt, and he was from Minnesota. We clicked immediately, knowing we would be experiencing our first year of college together.

While moving in, I met the guys across the hall. There was Shane from Idaho and Randy from Las Vegas. I was excited to see them carrying in skis. Parmalee was a co-ed dorm, and I couldn't believe I was going to be living in the same hallway as some of the cute girls moving in. Once all of my belongings were unloaded into my dorm room, I drove Garrett to the Denver airport for his flight back to Georgia.

# VAIL PASS

......................

I immediately became buddies with Randy and Shane across the hall. I loved that they had ski posters from the mid-1990s up on their dorm room walls. They mentioned they were planning to drive out to Vail to get season passes and asked if I wanted to join. I absolutely wanted a season pass for Vail, which was about a two-and-half-hour drive from Fort Collins. I called Dad to ask if he would help with the pass which was $300 as a student. Dad was all for it and wired the cash immediately. Shane offered to drive us to Vail in his old school Jeep Wagoneer with the wooded sides. Shortly into the trip, we broke out a joint, lit it up, and passed it around.

It was a gorgeous morning with the sun rising up over the mountains on I-70 as we made our way from Denver to Vail. I was still in awe that I was living in Colorado and these were my local mountains to explore. As we pulled into Vail, we asked around and found our way to the office where they issued season passes. I was pretty stoned as we filled out the required paperwork, posed for our season pass photos, and were handed our laminated passes. Once we had our passes, we headed back to Shane's Jeep. On the ride home, I realized that, in the excitement of everything, I had forgotten to pay for my pass as I still had the cash that Dad had given me in my wallet. I got nervous, thinking the Vail staff probably thought I intentionally walked out without paying.

When we got back to the dorm, I called the Vail office. When they answered, I deepened my voice, and said "This is Dennis Langley. I wanted to see if my son, Brett Langley, had stopped by to purchase a season pass with the money I had given him." The girl paused for a second, checking the status, and then said, "Yes, Mr. Langley, Brett came in earlier today, and he is all set." I decided to let it go as I could use the cash as a poor college kid and knew it would probably go fast, considering how expensive the lodges were at Vail.

# THE BROTHERHOOD

....................

Coming from the south, where the Greek system was a big part of college
life, I wanted to join a fraternity. I wanted the experience of becoming close
with a group of guys and have a house to call our own where we could throw
parties. When looking into it, I found out about Greek Golf; where a shuttle
bus would drive around to each of the fraternities, allowing you get a feel for
each of the houses. Each fraternity provided some sort of presentation about
who they were and why they were the best house on campus to join. After
touring all of the houses, I clicked with the guys at the Phi Delta Theta house
the most and put my focus on them. The Phi Delt house was a three-story
white brick house with black steel framed windows and to me was the best
looking fraternity house on campus. After attending a couple of their parties
to get to know them better, I was offered a bid to join their pledge class for
the fall of 1994.

It was great to have the fraternity house as a place to go since you couldn't
drink in the dorms. There was always something going on and a group of
guys hanging around the house. Tailgating for college football games was
always fun with everyone getting started early in the morning for game day.
I loved Hughes Stadium, built in the late '60s, it was a classic bowl stadium
with a grass berm above one of the end zones. The stadium was located just
outside of campus in a large open field right at the foothills of Horsetooth
Reservoir. It was one of the first college football stadiums ever to serve beer.
Fort Collins was known as a "micro-brew" capital having so many local independent beer breweries.

My first semester I was constantly back and forth between my dorm and
campus for class during the week. As the week would come to an end, I would

spend most of my time hanging around the fraternity house and looked forward to the house parties with our own bar in the basement. During pledgeship, I become really close with the guys in my class. The whole pledge program is designed to bring the class closer together, forming strong bonds in the group with everyone looking forward to becoming an active member and moving into the house. Some of my closest friends in life are guys who I went through the pledge program with during my freshman year.

Every now and then I would break away to go mountain biking. I had our local trails at Horsetooth Reservoir or the trails in Poudre Canyon which was about an hour away. The drive out to Poudre Canyon was beautiful with a narrow two-lane road that winded through the mountains alongside of the river. The mountain bike trails in Colorado were like Sope Creek on steroids, with longer trail systems, steeper hills and much more dramatic scenery with the mountains.

# HOMESICK

......................

It was a couple months into my freshman year when I had a moment where I suddenly became homesick. I had what seemed like a little panic attack thinking about how far I was away from family being half way across the country. I was alone in my dorm room one night, so I called Mom to talk about how I was feeling. Mom's voice really comforted me as she told me how proud she was of me and how it was completely normal to feel the way I did after such a big change in my life. She said I would be back in Atlanta soon enough for the Thanksgiving holidays and told me I could call her any time if I needed to talk. It was a very comforting conversation, and by the end, I wasn't sad or worried anymore. That conversation was a pivotal moment in my life that established my independence. After that discussion, I never felt homesick again. I felt after my move across the country for college, I was capable to move anywhere and do anything I desired moving forward.

# CADDY TRUNK CIGARETTES

......................

One day when I was returning from class, the front desk at my dorm told me I had a message. My friend Jay had called with a phone number where he could be reached. When I got to my room, I used my dorm phone to give him a call. He'd left his number to his room at the University of Michigan. It was great to hear Jay's voice and catch up on college life from different parts of the country. Jay asked if he could have my dad's number as he had recently come across a connection at an Indian reservation in New York where he could buy cases of cigarettes at an aggressive discount and wanted to see if my dad would be interested. I gave him Dad's home phone and told him to give him a call. I thought it was cool Jay had his own relationship with Dad.

Jay called Dad to tell him the scenario, and as soon as Dad figured out what Jay was talking about, he cut him off, saying he couldn't talk over the phone about this. He asked Jay to meet him at a local gas station by the house. Considering Dad's past, he didn't like to talk over the phone about anything outside of the straight and narrow. Dad met Jay at a local gas station by a pay phone to continue their discussion. Jay told Dad about his connection on the Indian reservation and offered to sell Dad cases of cigarettes for half the price of what he was normally buying them for. Jay mentioned it would help him out as he was paying his way through college. Dad told Jay he didn't need to know the details around how he was getting cigarettes at that price, and while he wouldn't be able to place any huge orders, he would do some smaller orders every couple of months. Dad told him when he returned from New York to let him know he was in town but not to mention any of the details over the phone. So every couple of months, Jay would rent a large Cadillac, drive to New York, and return with a trunk full of cigarettes. He would give Dad a heads-up that he was in town and stop by the house. Jay would back the Cadillac up to Dad's garage at the Davis Street house, pop the trunk, and let Dad buy as many cases as he felt comfortable with. Dad and Jay had a good little business arrangement where Dad could make a little more profit on cigarettes, and Jay earned a little extra cash for college.

# PULP FICTION

....................

For the holidays, I made plans to fly back to Georgia for Thanksgiving with Mom & Peter and then spend Christmas with Dad in Michigan. Thanksgiving was always my favorite time to be in Georgia with all of the leaves changing color and the cooler sweater weather. It was great to be back in town, catching up with old friends over drinks and exchanging stories about college life. I loved having home-cooked meals after eating dorm food all semester. That year Mom & Peter had a big Thanksgiving dinner catered for a large group of friends. The Buckhead house was always the best house for celebrations and parties.

While I was back in town, Mom & Peter took me by Tongue & Groove, which was a night club in Buckhead that had recently opened. When Peter had sold off his company, Mom's shares were with a lot of money. She wanted to sell some to invest in her own business. Mom invested in Tongue & Groove, owning a third of the business as a silent partner. It was an absolutely gorgeous nightclub and the first time I had ever been in an upscale bar. Up until that point, I had only been in college dive bars. Tongue & Groove catered to an older crowd, packed with successful business executives, professional athletes, and younger girls dressed to the nines. There was a large lounge area with couches and a cocktail bar where they played mellow house music. Then there was another smaller connected room with its own bar and dance floor where they played upbeat dance music. I thought it was so cool that Mom was one of the owners and we were treated like celebrities.

While hanging out with Mom in the club, she told me that she wanted to take me to a new movie that had just come out called *Pulp Fiction*. Mom loved movies and thought I would like it as it looked like something unique & cool. I was reluctant at first as I had never heard about it and didn't go to the movies much, but I wanted to spend some quality time with Mom. The next evening, Mom and I headed to one of the local theaters. Before we headed into the movie, I asked if she minded if I took a couple puffs off my one hitter before the movie. Mom didn't mind and stood there with me while I smoked in the parking lot.

From the opening scene, I was completely hooked into the movie and thought it was the coolest thing I had ever seen. It was so unique with the timing sequence being out of order. You had to piece the whole story together after you watched the whole movie. The characters, the dialogue, the music—everything about it was perfection. It was the most interesting thing I had ever seen, and I couldn't stop talking about it with Mom. I was so happy she suggested the movie; otherwise, I probably wouldn't have gone to see it on my own.

# COLORADO SKIING

.....................

As Christmas approached, I flew from Atlanta up to Detroit to spend a few weeks with Dad. As I rode the escalator down to the baggage claim, I could see Dad standing there at the bottom with his usual grin, happy to see me. I was looking forward to spending a few weeks at the Davis street house like old times. While at the baggage claim, I asked Dad about getting some skis for Christmas as I was planning to spend as much time as possible in Vail that winter since I had a season pass. Dad mentioned skis were expensive, so I would have to help him on the vending route while I was in town in exchange for the skis. It was fun to be back in the van with Dad, driving around to all of his customers. He loved to introduce me as his son who was home from college at Colorado State. I always liked seeing how much Dad had grown his business from when he had first started.

One of the surprises I had while in town was to challenge Dad to a game of racquetball. I knew how much he liked racquetball, so I had been taking a racquetball class as one of my electives but didn't tell him about it. While in the van, I nonchalantly asked him if he had played recently and suggested that we go play together while I was in town. I tried to act like it was no big deal, but in my mind, I couldn't wait to completely embarrass him at his own game. Dad said he hadn't played in years, but loved the idea, and said, "There is a club by the house. We could go play there."

The next day, we headed over to the courts, and as soon as we started playing, it was obvious things weren't going to go as planned. He was unbelievable and so much better than me. He had me running all over the court while he effortlessly stood in the same spot and put the ball wherever he wanted. He had this shot mastered where he would put the ball in the back corner, and I couldn't even fit my racquet into the corner to hit it. The ball would just die in the corner, and he racked up point after point with that shot. It was the same scenario from high school when I thought I could beat him in a running race out front of Grandma and Grandpa's house.

Right before Christmas, I had driven Dad crazy asking about the skis. There was a specific type of K2 skis I wanted, and I had called around to all of the local shops before finding a shop that had them. I told Dad there was a shop close by that had the exact skis I was looking for. He had enough of hearing about the skis, so we jumped in the van and headed to the ski shop. I got so excited seeing those K2 TNC skis in the rack. Dad got me a complete setup with boots, bindings, and poles. I could tell Dad enjoyed buying me the skis because he loved the sport and was happy to see me into it as well. I couldn't wait to get back to Fort Collins and head to Vail in the Jeep.

As the holiday break came to an end, Dad drove me to the Detroit airport to see me off back to college. We were talking about skiing, and Dad suggested we meet in Aspen that year for my spring break. It sounded like a perfect way to spend spring break and told Dad the dates so he could book his trip. He dropped me off at the airport, I gave him a hug and thanked him again for my skis. He gave me some extra cash to take back to school and told me how proud he was of me. We said our goodbyes and told him I looked forward to seeing him in Aspen in the spring.

Back on campus, I was back into my routine. I couldn't stop thinking about the movie *Pulp Fiction,* that Mom had taken me to over Thanksgiving, and went to the local theater to see it multiple times by myself. If I was looking for something to do, I would smoke a joint, go see it again and it never got old. I studied the film, picking up on new details each time and couldn't get enough of it.

I tried to get to Vail as often as possible but they were expensive day trips. Always on a budget, we would usually bring lunch and our own beer to tailgate in the parking lot. Vail was the ultimate ski resort to me, nothing beat those blue bird days in the back bowls and ending the day in the village for après-ski. The town of Vail is pure luxury. I loved browsing through the village ski shops checking out all of the expensive ski gear that I couldn't afford as a college kid.

I started hanging out a lot with one of the guys in my fraternity, Craig, who was a tall good-looking kid from Vancouver, Canada. Talking about skiing at one of our parties, he had skied a lot growing up living close to the resort, Whistler, so we planned a day trip to Vail together. When we met up in the morning to head to mountains, Craig was wearing a fancy purple-and-gold onesie ski suit. I was taken aback by his outfit at first. I joked that I didn't know if I could ski with him wearing that outfit all day as we both laughed. He shrugged it off and was like, "Whatever, man. Let's just get to the mountain." It turned out that Craig was a phenomenal skier, hitting the biggest jumps in the park and flying down the mountain with ease. As good of a skier as he was, he could wear whatever he wanted.

It was Spring Break in early March and everything was set to meet Dad in Aspen. He invited my cousin, Dave, who most of the family called "Little Dave" with his dad being "Big Dave". Dad didn't arrive in Aspen until a couple of days after the start of my break. Fort Collins had become a ghost town as all of the students had left for break. It always felt strange being on campus during the breaks without the usual student traffic. I was extremely low on cash, so I budgeted just enough for Taco Bell over those few days, putting the rest aside for gas money to Aspen. The day had come, I loaded my skis into the roof rack on the Jeep and hit the road for the six-hour drive to Aspen. I drove South on I-25, catching I-70 West in Denver. The drive from Denver to Vail on I-70 never disappointed, winding through the mountains.

I couldn't wait to see Dad and Little Dave. When I arrived at the hotel in Aspen, I told Dad how I had barely made it being completely broke. Dad laughed, gave me some cash, which put me at ease, and then took us out for a nice dinner in town. Afterward, we walked around shopping at the local ski shops and Dad bought me some new clothes for school.

The weather was absolutely perfect during our trip. Dad, Little Dave, and I skied the whole mountain, enjoying lunch on the slopeside patios, checking out the bars at the end of the day for après-ski, and then dinners at the best places in town. Considering I recently switched from snowboarding to skiing that year, Dad was impressed how comfortable I was on my skis. I told him how much I loved Vail and that he should plan another trip to ski Vail with me.

It was the last day of our trip when Dad realized we hadn't taken many photos. As we got off the chair lift at the top of one of the runs it had a perfect view of the mountains off in the distance and nobody else around. We decided to hang out and take some photos together. One of the first photos we took was of Dad and I, standing next to each other holding our skis, Dad's giving a thumbs up with the snow covered mountains blending into the white clouds amongst the blue skies in the background. It is my favorite photo I have of us together. Afterward, Dad wanted to get a bunch of photos that looked like multiple days of skiing, so we took turns changing jackets and hats amongst ourselves taking photos from different angles so Dad felt like he had a bunch of different photos from our trip. Looking through Dad's bin of photographs, he had all of the different variations of us from that photo session.

As the trip came to an end, Dad gave me some more cash to take back to college with me. I gave him a hug, told him how much I loved him, how much fun I had and hit the road back to Fort Collins.

# SUMMER OF '95

..................

As my freshman year came to an end, I finished my finals, packed up my dorm room and got ready to head back to Atlanta for the summer. Since I was moving into the fraternity house in the fall, I was able to store most of my stuff in an empty room at the house so I didn't have to take it with me for the drive cross-country and back. During the drive back to Atlanta I started to think about trading the Jeep for something that was more comfortable for long road trips back and forth to college. The Jeep was loud, rough, the hard top leaked during heavy rainstorms and since the seats didn't recline it was hard to sleep in if needed. Regardless, I made it back to the Buckhead house within a few days and was happy to be back in Atlanta for the summer.

I had only been at the house a few days before Jay called me to catch up and asked about coming down to visit. I was all for it and mentioned he should just stay the whole summer, but I needed to clear it with Mom & Peter first. When I brought it up to them, they were open to the idea as we had plenty of room, but laid down some ground rules. Jay would have to stay in my room to keep the guest room open for Mom & Peter's guests should they want to stay at the house. Jay would also would have to pay a small amount for rent each month to cover basic expenses and food. I called Jay back to run it by him, and he agreed to the conditions. We were both excited to spend the summer together hanging out in Georgia.

Jay showed up at the house within a few days with only a suitcase and his mountain bike. We needed to find jobs for the summer, so I asked Mom about maybe working at Tongue & Groove. Mom set up a meeting for me with one of the owners, Mark, to discuss it further. Mark owned multiple bars in Atlanta, and when I met with him, he discouraged me from working at Tongue & Groove, saying it catered to a much older crowd. He told me that I would have way more fun working at one of his other bars down the street called Odyssey's, which was a dive bar for young twentysomethings. He told me I was old enough to work as a bar back and I could make some good money on their busy nights. Mark explained the hours and how they were much different from a normal day job. He explained that I would be working ten hour shifts three to four days a week. He explained how I would need to arrive at 4:00 p.m. to set up and ice down the bars for the bartenders. Then I would have a gap of a couple of hours where I could leave, but needed to be back around 7:00 p.m. to assist the bartenders with whatever they needed to keep the drinks flowing until close at 4:00 a.m. and then cleanup. He explained the pay would be an hourly wage plus tips from the bartenders. He mentioned that they really only needed bar backs on busy nights, which were Thursday, Friday, and Saturday evenings.

During my first shift, I set up the bars, making sure all the liquor bottles were full enough to cover a night of drinks, cutting up lemons and limes, and icing down all the bottles of beer. When I came back later that evening at 7:00 p.m., I was nervous as it was going to be a long night, and I just wanted to do a good job. I was to support the bar on the upstairs outdoor patio. I had met the bartender a few times already, but it was my first night working with him. When I arrived, he told me that he had left something for me inside the cooler next to the beer. I wasn't sure what he was talking about, but I went into the cooler and found a glass bowl packed with weed and a lighter next to it. He'd left it for me to smoke to make the night less stressful and enjoy my shift. It was a fun job, hanging around a rowdy bar, listening to music, and watching everyone party till 4:00 a.m. The shift was long, but it would only be three days a week, and the cash payout at the end of the night made it all worth it. During those weekend nights I lived like a vampire sleeping in the day and at work all night.

Jay found a job as a waiter right away at a nice restaurant not that far from the house. We had so much fun that summer as roommates, living out of my bedroom with our own phone line and direct access to our room without going through the house. When our work schedules lined up and we were off at the same time, we always had something to do together, whether it was lounging by our pool, mountain biking my old trails at Sope Creek, or heading to a house party with my high school friends at night. We were introduced to this place called the Shoals, which was a hangout place on a large rock in the middle of the Chattahoochee River. It was fun to pack a small cooler, take the Jeep down to the river, walk through the waist-high water in Teva sport sandals to hang out with friends on the rock and drink. When you got too hot from the Georgia heat, you just jumped in the river to cool off. If we had a couple of beers, we took the backroads all the way back to the house, which were these winding two-lane roads covered by trees. Those roads are still some of the most beautiful roads I have ever driven on. Later in life, Jay told me a lot of people talk about listening to Pink Floyd's *Darkside of the Moon* as being one of their most memorable music experiences, but for him it was driving in the Jeep with the top down on those winding roads that summer, blasting Smashing Pumpkins' *Siamese Dream* through my 6X9 speakers mounted on the back wheel wells.

That summer, we got tickets to an Allman Brothers show at Lakewood Amphitheater. One of my friends, Cheech, drove us that day in his Volkswagen Bus and we ended up coming across some mushrooms tailgating in the parking lot before the show. The band came on mid-afternoon and we found our spot on the lawn in the back section of the venue. It doesn't get much better than sitting on the grass at Lakewood Amphitheater during a hot sunny Georgia day, listening to Duane Allman and the band jam. As the mushrooms kicked in, Jay and I wanted to see if we could get closer to the stage. We were standing against this waist-high railing with a bouncer right next to us checking tickets for admittance down to the assigned seats in front of the stage. As some people with tickets came up to the bouncer, he turned his back to us and was distracted. Jay and I looked at each other, thinking the same thing, and immediately hopped over the little fence behind the bouncer's back, walked down to the crowd, and blended in with them. We had third row seats for the remainder of the show. The band played well into the evening, and once the show came to an end, we jumped in Cheech's bus to head back to the house.

The party came to an end toward the end of the summer when my grades from my freshman year showed up at the house. They were much worse than I had anticipated, and Peter was furious. We had a heated discussion, and he said he wasn't going to pay half of my out-of-state college tuition for grades like that, and he was done. It was the first year I had gotten such poor grades. I was really disappointed with myself but knew I could do better. I went to my room and called Dad to tell him the news. Dad was really disappointed as well, but he really wanted me to graduate college. I explained to him how it was a big adjustment my first year, moving cross-country, trying to meet new friends and get situated. He asked if I thought I could get through it and still graduate in the next three years. I convinced him that I could. Dad told me when the summer was over to drive back out to Colorado and focus on school. He said he would pay for the rest of my college tuition, but I would have to get a part-time job to help. I agreed to the plan and was so grateful he provided an opportunity for me to turn things around and complete my college education.

In the final weeks of summer, Jay and I made plans for a road trip back to Colorado. Jay wanted to join me, spend a few days in Fort Collins, and then fly back before the start his fall semester at University of Michigan. We wanted to make our trip a memorable adventure. We decided to take the southern route stopping in New Orleans, heading across Texas and then up through New Mexico.

Considering our upcoming trip, I decided it was time to look into trading the Jeep towards something better suited for driving cross-country. I brought up the idea to Mom & Peter, explaining how I wanted to get something more comfortable for long road trips. Initially Mom & Peter weren't big on the idea, but they decided to leave it up to me, and I would have to sell it all on

my own. I listed my Jeep in the local Autotrader for $9,000, which is what
Mom & Peter originally bought it for. In looking for my next vehicle, I found
a used two-door white Isuzu Trooper RS at the local Land Rover dealership
and thought it was perfect. It was a similar type of vehicle as my Jeep but
would be more comfortable, have more room and drive better on the road.
The Trooper was listed for $9,000 as well.

I knew my Jeep was one of the nicer ones around, and I wanted to get
top dollar for it.

I had multiple people interested, and held firm on my asking price. I met
with this family who wanted to meet at a local gas station to take a look at
the Jeep. They were considering Jeeps for their son, and I could tell he was in
love with it as soon as he saw it. He had an older brother who kept pointing
out minor issues and flaws as a way to negotiate the price down. I didn't ac-
knowledge any of his comments as any real issues as it was a used Jeep. I finally
had enough and said I needed to get going; the price was $9,000 if they were
interested, and they became flustered at the potential of losing the Jeep. They
told me they wanted it and paid cash at full asking price. Mom and Peter were
so impressed how I handled the whole situation, getting the same amount
of money they had bought the Jeep for a few years earlier, considering all the
miles I had put on it between high school and driving to Colorado and back.

With cash in hand, it was time to negotiate on the Isuzu Trooper. I offered
the seller $8,000, planning to use the remaining $1,000 toward a roof rack
and new stereo with a CD player. The seller wasn't thrilled with the offer, but
I stayed calm and told him that was all I could spend. He told me he would
have to get back to me, and I eagerly awaited to hear back from him. He called
the next day and accepted my offer. Mom dropped me off at the Land Rover
dealer, and I worked through the paperwork, paying for the truck in cash.

I immediately drove my new Trooper over to REI to get it fitted for a
roof rack to carry my bike, skis, and a cargo basket for any extra luggage for
our trip to Colorado. The REI was right by my high school, so I stopped by,
looking at my old school and thinking about how much my life had changed

in just one year since graduation. Within days, I had the new stereo installed, and we were ready for our trip back to Fort Collins.

Jay and I were ready to get on the road. As we were packing, Peter approached Jay and said he had something for him. Peter handed Jay back the money he had collected as rent over the summer and said he just wanted to see what type of person his son was hanging out with. Peter told Jay they really enjoyed having him stay with us that summer and was welcome any time. Jay was so grateful to have some extra cash for our trip. With the Trooper packed, I hugged Mom & Peter as we said our goodbyes and hit the road to New Orleans.

The drive from Atlanta to New Orleans was about seven hours. We arrived late afternoon and were excited to explore Bourbon Street. We walked up and down the street and in and out of different bars, listening to live music and drinking well into the night. I was uncomfortable that I had all of the cash I had made at the bar over the summer for college in my pocket. I told Jay I wanted to head back to the Trooper and lock up my cash in the glove box. Afterward, I felt so relieved not having so much cash on me. It was shortly after we were hanging out in front one of the bars when a guy approached us, making small talk. He asked where we from and welcomed us to New Orleans. In the discussion, he mentioned there was a park close by that was a great place to smoke a joint and we should check it out while in town. He was mainly talking with Jay as I was skeptical of the guy and the whole situation. Jay didn't think there was anything to worry about. He said, "Let's go check out this park," so I followed along.

As we got further away from Bourbon Street, the more uncomfortable I became as we were in a rough area and it didn't seem like there would be any beautiful parks close by. I dropped back, letting Jay and the guy continue to talk while I took a twenty dollar bill from my pocket and stuffed it down the top of my sock. I could see the guy glanced back at me to see what I was up to, but I didn't think he saw what I was doing. I then told them that I didn't want to go any further and wanted to get back to Bourbon Street. The guy suggested we just smoke right there on the front steps of a townhouse.

I walked up a few steps and was sitting with my back to the front door with Jay and the guy a few steps below me. We were all kind of blocked in by the brick railings on the sides of the staircase. The guy pulled some weed from his pocket and asked for a bill to roll up a joint. I handed over a dollar, and the guy said this wouldn't work as he needed something bigger. At that point, we knew what was going on. I told him that was all I had on me. The guy stood up, facing me, and put his hand behind his back, making it look like he had something tucked in his back waistband. He said, "We can do this the easy way or the hard way." I kept to my story that the dollar was all that I had. The guy became frustrated and said, "What about the other bill you stuffed in your sock while we were walking here?"

I pulled the twenty dollar bill from my sock and handed it to him. I insisted that was really all I had. The guy insisted that we must have more since we were driving cross-country. Trying to convince him, I pulled everything from my pockets, showing him my keys and empty wallet. The guy grabbed my keys out of my hand, which changed the situation as Jay and I realized we would be stranded without our keys to the Trooper. Jay and I were now ready to stand up for ourselves. I stood firm, telling the guy he had everything and should leave us alone. He threw my keys down the street and ran off in the other direction. I walked over to grab my keys and was so upset that we had gotten ourselves into that situation. As we walked back to Bourbon Street, I kept saying how stupid I felt, how much I hated New Orleans and didn't want to stay the night. The rush of adrenaline had sobered us up, so we decided to get some food and get back on the road to San Antonio, taking turns driving throughout the night.

When we made it to San Antonio, we were exhausted from taking turns driving all night and wanted to get some sleep. We checked into this old Spanish-style hotel and pretty much slept the whole day. Around dinnertime, we got cleaned up and decided to check out the town before leaving in the morning. We walked around the shops on the San Antonio River Walk and found a really good Mexican restaurant for dinner.

In the morning, we packed a little cooler with some basic snacks of chips, salsa, apples, cold cuts to make some sandwiches and got back on the road. It took a full day to just drive across Texas and the muggy heat was unbearable. The air-conditioning in the Trooper was no match for the heat, and it almost felt better to just drive with the windows down to feel the wind blowing through the cabin. We made it to White Sands, New Mexico, and checked into a local motel to get some sleep.

The next morning, we headed over to the dunes. We climbed the biggest one we could find, smoked a joint, and took in the view with no one else in sight. There was a large wooden chair that must have been fifty feet tall off in the distance. It was such an unusual sight out in the middle of nowhere that we questioned if we were hallucinating from the joint and unbearable heat. We spent a few hours hanging out and taking photos. We got back on the road to finish our final stretch of the trip to Fort Collins, which was about a ten-hour drive.

Jay drove through most of southern Colorado while I rode shotgun with my window down, looking at the mountains and thinking about how excited I was to start my sophomore year back at Colorado State. We arrived at my fraternity house late that night. There were only a handful of guys staying at the house over the summer, so we had multiple rooms to choose from. We found a smaller room on the third floor with bunk beds that we claimed as our own until school started in which rooms would be determined based on tenure in the house. I loved having Jay in Fort Collins and showing him around my college town. We went hiking in Horsetooth and swam in the reservoir.

One of the nights, someone at the house had some mushrooms, so we decided to hike up to a peak in Horsetooth to take them and have a couple of beers. While hanging out on the mountaintop taking in the view, a massive thunderstorm rolled in suddenly. It was beautiful to see the lightning light up the reservoir for a brief second in the mountains, but then the heavy rain started instantly. We were all immediately soaked and started hiking quickly back down to the car. We made it back to house, and the mushrooms had kicked in. Everyone wanted to continue hanging out, so we put some music on in one of the third-floor rooms, put on rain jackets with the hoods up, and hung out on the sundeck, drinking beers in the rain.

It was only a few days away from the start of the school year, and Jay needed to get back to start his semester at University of Michigan. I drove him to the Denver airport, talking about how fun our summer was together, and I saw him off back to Detroit.

# LOVE AT FIRST SIGHT

......................

When everyone was back from the summer break, rooms were decided in the fraternity house. I got one of the larger rooms on the third floor that I would be sharing with a guy named Tony from Vermont. Tony had a girlfriend in the dorms, so there were many nights when I had the room to myself. I loved falling asleep at night, watching snowboarding videos with the sound off while playing Nirvana's *Unplugged* album. That album paired with images of guys carving through deep powder snow and the sound of my little space heater to keep the room warm because of the old poorly insulated windows was so relaxing to me. I found a job at local hotel, setting up events for banquets, weddings, and corporate events. It was very flexible, which was great to accommodate time off for breaks and the holidays. Living in the fraternity house was fun as there was always something going on or someone to hang out with in one of the rooms. Considering all of the distractions and working part-time, I became better at managing my time to keep my grades up. I had made an agreement with Dad that I would graduate in three years, and I didn't want to let him or myself down on that promise.

Wednesday nights became a thing as a group of us liked to go over to this old cheesy nightclub called Tangz. It was an eighteen and over club but those twenty-one and older could drink. If you were under twenty-one, you got a mark on your hand at the door that was easily washed off in the bathroom once you were inside. They had an event called Bladder Busters where the bathrooms were taped off at the start of the night, and the beer flowed for free until the first person of the night broke through the tape to use the bathroom. There were stories of people peeing under the tables or doing whatever it took to relieve themselves so everyone could drink as much as possible for free.

If you were the guy who busted through the tape that night, you probably weren't going home with anyone as it wasn't a good look. There was a large saltwater fish tank that separated the pool table area from the dance floor. I loved that bar and became a regular.

I was there every Wednesday that semester, right up until the last one when I came down with a bad cold and didn't want to get out of bed. My buddy Adam knew how much I loved Wednesday nights, so he came into my room, sat at the end of my bed, and gave me a pep talk. He told me I would look back on this decision later in life and regret that I made it to Tangz every Wednesday night except for the very last one. He asked me if I would be able to live with that for the rest of my life. I was motivated by his speech. I said, "You're right," flung the blanket off me, got out of bed to get ready, and went to Tangz that night. I can honestly say I was there every Wednesday in the fall of '95.

A couple months into my spring semester, I was at Tangz one night when I saw one of the prettiest girls I had ever seen. I became frozen as this thin, long-legged, dirty blonde with supermodel looks wearing tight jeans and a fur collar jacket walked through the door. She was absolutely gorgeous, and I couldn't keep my eyes off her as she walked through the bar. As she walked by, we made eye contact briefly, but there didn't seem to be much interest from her. I typically didn't approach girls until I felt some sort of a positive reaction first which I didn't get. The night had come and gone without talking to her. I left the bar that night thinking she was out of my league but I couldn't stop thinking about her and hoped to see her again.

Shortly after my fraternity was hosting a date night function at a restaurant in the mountains. We had a bus chartered to shuttle us to and from the event. I was set up on a blind date with a girl who was friends with one of the sorority girls dating a guy in my fraternity. My obsession with Quentin Tarantino movies continued and I was really into his earlier film *Reservoir Dogs*. I wanted to dress like one of the gangsters in the movie for our event. I wore a black suit with a plain white dress shirt with the collar open. As I boarded the bus for the event, I saw the girl from Tangz sitting in one of the seats and was filled with excitement. As I walked by, we locked eyes a little longer, and I got the type of reaction I had hoped for but worried she was now dating someone else in my fraternity. As the night went on, I tried not to make my interest in her obvious, but I asked around about her. Her name was Jennifer, and she was set up on a blind date for the event just as I was. There were a lot of people at the event, and the night finished without any interaction as we were both preoccupied with our dates.

A few nights later, I was studying in my room with the door open when Jennifer walked by with a group of girls. I couldn't believe she was in our house on a random weekday evening without any events going on. I could hear the girls hanging out in one of the rooms down the hall. I decided to head down and join the conversation. After introducing myself to Jennifer, we kept making eye contact. As part of the discussions, I told a story about growing up in Atlanta and had Jennifer's complete attention. I wasn't able to stay for long as I had a test the next day, so I said goodbye to the group. I strutted back down the hall to my room with an overwhelming sense of happiness as I felt I had turned a corner with Jennifer.

The following Wednesday night, I headed over to Tangz with a group of guys. Jennifer walked through the door with a group of her friends. We saw each other, but I was trying to play it cool and not make it so obvious I was crazy about her. One of my buddies had enough of the cool guy attitude and decided to speed up the process. He walked up to Jennifer and her friends and invited them over to hang out. As our groups mingled together, Jennifer and I connected immediately. I was completely oblivious as to what was going on outside of hanging out with her. We talked for most of the night, getting to know each other, and as the night came to an end, we made plans for me to pick her up at her dorm that Friday for a dinner date.

The night of our first date, I drove over to Jennifer's dorm, which was in these two identical towers that looked like office buildings; they were the tallest buildings on campus. I made my way up to her room on one of the top floors. As she answered the door, she invited me in to meet her roommate and see their room. I immediately loved the fact that Jennifer had a poster of the movie *Pulp Fiction* on her wall, and I told her how crazy I was about that movie. Her roommate had a Pearl Jam poster up, so it was fair to say I loved their taste in movies and music. We decided on dinner at Coopersmith's, which was popular tavern, in Old Town Fort Collins. After dinner, we hung out in my room late into the night, continuing to get to know each other sharing stories from our past.

After our first date, we were a couple, spending most of our nights together and meeting up on campus in between classes when our schedules lined up. I loved staying with Jennifer in her dorm and waking up next to the window with a perfect view of Horsetooth Mountain. Later in life, Jennifer told me it was the way I was dressed when I boarded the shuttle bus for our fraternity date function wearing a black suit with an open white collared shirt that drew her attention to me. She told me that she loved my houndstooth flannel with the elbow patches, that I wore often, as it was different than how guys typically dressed.

Jennifer & I spent our last few months of my sophomore year together. As the summer break approached, we discussed our plans. Jenn would be heading back to her parents' house in Denver for the summer while I had planned to stay in Fort Collins. We knew we wouldn't be able to see each other often, so we put our relationship on pause to pick things back up once school resumed in the fall.

As the school year was coming to an end, three of my fraternity brothers—Adam, Craig, Dave—and I decided we wanted to move into our own place in the fall since we were spending most of our time together. Adam had just gotten his real estate license as part of his focus on construction management and found us a new construction small four-bedroom house that was to be finished right before the school year started. We loved the idea of having our own place together and signed a one-year lease on the house. We agreed the rooms would be first-come, first-served based on whoever made it back to Fort Collins before the start of the school year.

# ON THE ROAD

.................

Fort Collins became a ghost town in the summer as most of the students headed home for the break. The hotel I worked at slowed way down; they didn't have many events booked during the summer months. My manager told me that with so few hours of available work, I could take a few months off and enjoy the summer break. I called Dad to tell him the scenario and asked if he would help me through the summer as I wanted to spend some time on the road. I told him one of my friends Randy was renting a place in Los Angeles for the summer and invited me to come visit for a few weeks. Dad thought it sounded cool and wired some cash to support my trip. I packed up the Trooper and hit the road. It was about a fifteen-hour drive to Los Angeles, taking me through the Rocky Mountains, across Utah and through Las Vegas. I loved being back on the road with my one-hitter, listening to music and checking out the western states. I didn't want to spend money on a hotel room, so I slept in my truck on the side of the road just east of Las Vegas. It was hot and muggy in the desert, so when I woke up, I found a local motel to jump in their pool to refresh myself before getting on the road for the final leg of my trip to Los Angeles. I arrived at Randy's apartment, which was in Westwood, where the campus of UCLA is located and close to Beverly Hills.

Los Angeles was the epitome of cool to me. Outside of being known for where all of the movie stars and famous musicians lived, I thought it was cool because a lot of my childhood bike and skateboard idols were from California. Driving down the famous Sunset Strip in person for the first time had such a mystique to it. One night, through one of Randy's friends, we got V.I.P. passes to the upstairs lounge at the House of Blues in West Hollywood. Being nineteen years old and hanging out in the lounge made me feel like we were celebrities. The weather was perfect every day, we spent a few days on Venice and Santa Monica Beach. The Pacific Ocean was always much colder than it looked. I loved the laid back vibe of the beach towns. Most of the time we just hung around the pubs and restaurants in Westwood, which felt much more prestigious compared to our college town of Fort Collins.

Toward the end of my trip, I was walking down to the music store in Westwood and stopped into a little gift shop. I found a postcard with a photo of Brad Pitt and thought it would be cool to send to Jennifer. I wrote her a short message about my trip out to Los Angeles and mailed it out to her. As much as I enjoyed my stay in California, it was time to make my way back to Colorado.

When I arrived back in Fort Collins, I checked in at the hotel where I worked to see if anything had changed, but things were the same. I really liked being on the road, so I called Dad to ask if I should head to Detroit to spend some time with him. He loved the idea and wired me some more cash for my trip. I got some rest at the fraternity house, repacked the Trooper, replenished my dugout and got back on the road heading east toward Detroit. The drive east of Colorado wasn't as pretty, but I still liked seeing the whole country and was excited to spend some time with Dad.

As I arrived, Dad met me out in the driveway, excited to see me. It was a nice change of pace being in Michigan during the summer with nice weather as I usually visited during the winter Holidays. It was a mellow and relaxing couple of weeks. During the day we would jump in the work van so I could help on the vending route. I told him all about my trip out to Los Angeles and how cool I thought it was out there. In the evenings, Dad would cook dinner for us on the grill in the backyard. It was always fun being back at the Davis Street house. My room was still the same as when I lived there my first couple years of high school. Being in that room always made me reflect on how much had changed in my life. I stayed with Dad for about three weeks before it was time to start making my way back to Fort Collins. I hugged Dad goodbye, thanked him for everything, told him how great it was to spend some time together over the summer and got back on the road.

When I reached Denver, I stopped by a gas station pay phone just off the highway to try and reach Jenn at her parent's house. Her mom answered, I introduced myself as a friend of Jenn's and asked if she was home. Her mom said she was at work and would let her know I called. I was anxious to get back to Fort Collins so I got back on the highway for the final hour of my trip.

# WHITCOMB STREET HOUSE

......................

As the summer came to an end, I packed up my room in the fraternity house and moved over to our new little house on Whitcomb Street. Dave & I were the first two to be back in Fort Collins before the start of school so we got our first pick on rooms in the house. I claimed an upstairs bedroom that overlooked the front entrance, which faced an alleyway. I was excited to start my junior year in the fall of 96 with the boys.

Just before school started, Jennifer had arrived back in Fort Collins. I invited her to join my roommates and I to go see a movie called *Trainspotting*, which was an edgy and vulgar movie about a group of young British guys experimenting with heroin. Considering our time apart over the summer, I wasn't sure where things stood in our relationship. Jennifer was not a fan of the movie, and it wasn't the best choice for a date night. I should have just kept it a guys' night out. When we got back to the house, I could tell Jennifer was turned off by the whole situation, hanging out with us while we laughed and joked during such a vulgar movie. We got into an argument over the situation back at the house, which sent us on our own separate paths to start the school year.

The fall semester was underway, and I was working my usual twenty hours a week at the hotel. I had completed most of my core requirements, and it was time to focus on a major. I was still very much obsessed with movies, but Colorado State didn't have a full-blown film school. Their film and media classes were within speech communications. I decided that would be my focus and felt a speech communications degree was also a broad degree that could apply to many professions if my dreams as a filmmaker didn't pan out.

That semester, my roommates and I started to fade away from hanging around the fraternity house. We were a pretty tight group and just wanted to hang out with each other at our place. I thought it was cool we were all from different places. Adam was from the Bay Area in California; Craig was from Vancouver, Canada; and Dave was from Dublin, Ireland. We formed our strong bonds as part of joining the fraternity together, but we felt like the house belonged to the younger class now, who moved in just as we had the previous year. Dave brought home a black lab puppy he named Seamus, and it was fun to have a little playful puppy running around the house. We had a little backyard area for parties and barbeques when the weather was nice. We lived a block away from a liquor store, so we had easy access to keep the refrigerator stocked with beers.

One day when I was walking back from class, I saw Dave's car still running in a parking space while he ran inside to grab some beers. I hopped in his car, drove it around the corner out of sight, and hid, waiting to watch his reaction when he came out. He walked out with his little micro-brew six-pack, in shock his car was nowhere to be found. In a state of panic, he asked another customer waiting in their car if they had seen anyone drive off in his old bronze-colored Oldsmobile Cutlass Sierra, but they hadn't seen anything. He looked around for a few seconds, then overwhelmed with frustration, let out a loud "Fuck!" He was a stocky, tough guy, and we always thought it was funny when he lost his cool. Like when he came home one-day, after doing bad on a test, and flung his backpack through his bedroom wall. I walked around the corner, calling out to him, and as soon as he saw me standing there with a smile on my face, he knew what had happened. We laughed about the scenario as we jumped in his car around the corner and drove back to the house together.

We all got along really well and were constantly entertained by our back-and-forth banter with each other. We were always in and out of the house for class with the campus a short walk away. We had settled into our routines and were enjoying college life in our own little house together.

During the Holiday break I was back in Detroit to spend some time with Dad. The morning of Christmas Eve, we woke up to a complete whiteout. It had snowed hard overnight and continued through the morning. It was the perfect day to relax together at the house. I suggested we smoke a joint and watch the movie *Dazed and Confused*. Dad wasn't big into movies, so I had to convince him. I explained the movie was about a group of high school kids from the mid-1970s, and told him he would like the music, cars, and clothing taking him back to his younger years. We grabbed some blankets and pillows to get comfortable on the couch and lit up a joint as I started the movie. I could tell from the opening scene with Aerosmith's "Sweet Emotion" playing while one of the muscle cars pulled into the high school parking lot in slow motion that Dad was hooked. I remember thinking how cool it was that I had the type of relationship with Dad that was more like hanging out with one of my buddies where we could smoke and watch movies together. I could tell he loved the movie as it probably reminded him a lot of his younger years, and he thought the girls were pretty. It was a memorable morning being snowed in at the Davis Street house spending a unique Christmas Eve together.

In March of 1997, Peter's son, Peter Jr., who was a documentary filmmaker living in Los Angeles, had one of his documentaries called *Rhyme & Reason* picked up by Miramax Films and released in the theaters. Peter Jr. was nominated for an Academy Award in 1993 for an earlier documentary he made called *Blood Ties: The Life and Work of Sally Mann*. Peter Jr.'s latest documentary *Rhyme & Reason* captured late '90s Hip-hop music and culture. I couldn't believe the film was actually showing at a local theater in Fort Collins and went to see it right away. I was so proud of what Peter had accomplished. I thought it was so cool that it was released through Miramax, which was the same company that released *Pulp Fiction*.

Just like *Pulp Fiction*, I had gone to see *Rhyme and Reason* multiple times in our local theater. I recommended the film to all my friends and even my film teacher, who went to see it. The film brought me back to my love for Hip-hop and introduced me to a whole new obsession with the Wu-Tang Clan, which was a rap group of nine members, that were all individually phenomenal. They had a unique sound incorporating movie clips and sword fighting sound effects sampled from old Kung-Fu movies.

In the years leading up to the release of *Rhyme & Reason*, Peter would ask my opinion on various hip-hop artists as he knew I was really into it in the late '80s through early '90s. I never gave his questions about various artists much thought, but I had no idea how big of a deal his film would become. Considering Peter's background as a lead guitarist in an '80s hair band, I liked to joke with him that he knew nothing about hip-hop, so how could he make a documentary on it? Shortly after the release of the film, Peter sent me an autographed *Rhyme & Reason* poster that I had framed and hung up in the living room at our Whitcomb Street house. I loved the photo of Method Man from Wu-Tang on the poster and was always proud to talk about it at our house parties. *Rhyme and Reason* was such an inspiration as Peter's accomplishment made me feel my dreams of one day making a film were a possibility.

# CALIFORNIA DREAMIN'

......................

As the school year came to end, I planned to spend a mellow summer in Fort Collins before the start of my senior year. Dad agreed to help me through the summer months as he understood how my job at the hotel slowed way down that time of year. I thought a great way to occupy myself that summer would be to find a Super8 Camera and spend time developing my passion for filmmaking. In my search, I came across a silver vintage camera at a local pawn shop that I fell in love with that was in perfect shape. My grandparents, who were retired in Florida, had an old Super8 projector in their garage that they were happy to give to me as they no longer had use for it.

During this time, Jay shared the same passion and was enrolled in University of Michigan's film program. We would write each other handwritten letters back and forth, talking about our inspirations and latest creative efforts with our little film projects. Working with Super8 film was time-consuming. I really had to plan out what I wanted to shoot. The film was expensive, and there was no way to see the footage until it was developed, which was a long process. I had to ship the film out of state and wait weeks to get it back. My Super8 camera didn't have sound, so I focused on capturing cool images or clips that I could match up with music. I was creating little experimental art films. I experimented with different images set to a wide variety of music that included The Beatles, DJ Shadow, The Orb and Wu-Tang. I liked playing around with time lapses showing a sequence of events happen very quickly. One morning, I got permission from the hotel I worked at to get on the roof and film a time lapse of the sunrise over Fort Collins.

For the sound in my films, I used my double tape deck on my stereo to record the soundtrack. I wanted to make my bedroom, which was my studio, more interesting, so I painted my walls brick red. I had candles everywhere for softer lighting. I taped up a large white poster board to the back of my bedroom door and used it as a screen to project my films. I found this young guy who opened a film editing studio in a small room at a local UPS store. I would take in my raw footage and music so he could transfer to VHS tape making it easier to show my friends. That summer, I had my Super8 with me everywhere as I looked for interesting things to film.

As the summer came to an end, my roommates rolled back into town and got situated in the house. Everyone was excited to start our final year of college together before heading out into the real world. My mind was focused on graduating and moving on to the next chapter in my life. I had my routine down between school, working at the hotel, and continuing to experiment with my little film projects. After graduation, I wanted to move to Los Angeles and find my way in the film industry. I took comfort in the fact that Peter Jr. was already out there and would be someone I could go to for advice and guidance. I was attracted to California and focused on moving to Hollywood as soon as possible.

After I had a bunch of little experimental film clips from the summer, I wanted to create a final cohesive piece. It was a time-consuming process of splicing and taping together the segments by hand to create a final cut and the timing up the music separately to match. We were having regular parties at our house, and I thought it would be cool to premiere my little film at one of them on my bedroom screen. My final cut wasn't anything super impressive, but it was something I was proud of, and I thought it showcased my creative style at the time as an early filmmaker.

In my final semester, I was excited that the finish line was near and I would be graduating in the summer of 1998. One of my favorite classes that semester was a creative writing class. I wrote a story about a day in the life with my roommates in our little house. I took our funniest moments over the past few years along with all of our typical back-and-forth banter and wrote it as if it all happened as part of a typical day. When I read my story to the class, I enjoyed how much it made everyone laugh, and got such a positive reaction from my teacher. He made me feel like I had something with my writing. I had great content to work with as we were a pretty funny group of guys. I got an A in the class, and it was fun to recap the last few years of my college experience.

As we approached graduation, my parents made their travel plans to spend a few days in Fort Collins celebrating my accomplishment. My roommates and I rented out a local pub called Sullivan's to host all of our family and friends for a big party after the ceremony. I invited Jay, and Dad picked up his hotel room for his stay while in Fort Collins. The night before the graduation ceremony, we had a party at our place with all of our parents. It was fun to see them all hanging out together while we shared stories of living together over the past few years.

The day of the ceremony, it was gorgeous outside, and everyone was so excited putting on their caps and gowns on at the house. Sitting among the graduation class, I loved seeing Dad, Mom, and Peter sitting together. After the ceremony, I walked over them, and seeing Dad up close, I could tell he had been crying. He was so proud of my accomplishment and graduating within four years. During our discussions, Peter and Mom told me that for my graduation present, they were going to provide a monthly allowance over the next year to support me during my internship with Peter Jr. in Hollywood. They told me that they thought it would have taken me five years to get through college, so they were going to treat the next year as if I were continuing with my education. They emphasized that it would only be for a year, so I would have to figure out how to become self-sufficient by the end of the year. I hugged them all and was looking forward to the next chapter in my life.

I was ready to celebrate, so we made our way back to our house to get changed and head over to Sullivan's for our graduation party. As the night went on, the bar became more and more packed with familiar faces. Jennifer stopped by to join the celebration. She ended up standing next to Dad at the bar while waiting to get a drink. Dad thought she was stunning, struck up a conversation with her and asked how she knew me. Jenn told him that she used to be my girlfriend. Dad asked how I could have ever broken up with someone as pretty as her and picked up the drinks for Jenn and her friends.

Later that night, I looked across the room and saw Peter hanging out at the bar by himself. I walked over and asked where Mom was. Peter said, "She went out to the car with your dad for a bit." I smiled as I knew what was probably going on. I imagined them sitting in the Corvette together before heading to the Elton John concert in the '70s. Over the years after the divorce, Mom and Dad had somewhat of a rocky relationship, but after that night, it seemed as though they had made amends and were able to put the past behind them.

The celebration went on well past midnight until they eventually had to shut the party down. My roommate Dave and I decided to walk home as one of our final trips across campus, and invited Dad to join us. As we walked across campus, we shared stories with Dad about our college experience. We stopped by the outdoor tables at the student center, which provided an awesome view of Horsetooth Mountains to smoke a joint. We talked about our plans after college, and I mentioned how excited I was to move to Hollywood to pursue my passion for filmmaking. Dad was always supportive of me chasing my dreams but was skeptical as to how I was going to make a living from it. He responded with, "you're dreaming," but he knew I would figure out my way in life.

# HOLLYWOOD

. . . . . . . . . . . . . . . . . . .

Everything was packed in my Trooper, and I couldn't wait to get on the road to Hollywood. My roommates and I said our goodbyes with no plans as to when we would see each other again. I hit the road and almost made it to the Nevada border when it became a struggle to shift my truck into gear. I pulled off the highway into a little town and found a service shop to have them take a look. They said my clutch was blown and would need to be replaced. They recommended that I try to make it to Las Vegas a few hours away as I would have a much better chance of getting a new clutch faster considering Vegas is a much larger city. With the clutch blown, I got back on the highway, having to shift at the perfect moment to get it into the next gear.

I managed to make it to Vegas and pulled off the first exit into a gas station. I looked for a local service station in the phone book hanging from a pay phone. I called a shop that had one of the larger ads and told them my situation. The guy said I would have to bring it in so they could take a look at it. I pulled into a junky little shop with old cars, used tires, and parts everywhere. I checked in and took a seat in the tiny waiting room. It was sweltering hot without air-conditioning and a cheap fan blowing hot air around.

While I was waiting for them to look at my truck, this girl strutted through the door wearing a short black leather miniskirt, high heels and carrying a little boom box. The mechanics guided her into the manager's office across the lobby and closed the door behind them. Shortly after, the music started up but was muffled behind the closed door. The guys were hootin' and hollerin' having what sounded like a great time inside the closed-door meeting. About ten minutes later, the door opened, and they all filtered out following the girl with these embarrassed looks on their faces as they walked by me, a sweaty mess, in the waiting room. The manager was the last one out, who looked disheveled, with his thinning hair all messed up. He felt obligated to tell me that wasn't a usual thing, but it was his birthday, so the guys planned a little surprise for him.

After taking a look at my truck, they confirmed I needed a new clutch and said it would take them a few days to locate the part and get it installed. I didn't have much of choice, as my truck was pretty much undriveable. I found a motel close by, and one of the mechanics gave me a ride over. There could have been much worse places to be stuck than in Vegas. I spent the next few days relaxing by the motel pool during the day and checking out some of the nightclubs on the strip at night. When I picked up my truck, the bill was shockingly expensive and a completely unexpected setback, but I needed to get back on the road, so I had no choice but to put it on a credit card.

I arrived in Westwood at my friend Randy's apartment where I was going to stay for a week or so while I looked for my own place. In my search, I found a room for rent within a few days that was in a white stucco Spanish-style house in East Hollywood on Wilton Street between Hollywood Boulevard and Franklin Avenue. The large house had been broken up into individual studio rooms for rent with a common shared kitchen area. I liked the room for rent because it had its own private entrance and wood floors. The house wasn't in a great area, but it was in Hollywood, where I wanted to be, and the rent was reasonable. I envisioned Hollywood to be much more glamorous than how it was in reality. Hollywood Boulevard was pretty sketchy with homeless people, drugs, and hookers. My room was a short drive down the famous Sunset Strip to Peter Jr.'s house and his film studio on the corner of Sunset Boulevard and Crescent Heights.

I immediately scheduled a time to stop by Peter's studio and see when I could start my internship. I thought his studio was so cool with multiple displays in the editing rooms, libraries of video tapes, and posters on the wall of Peter's films along with some of his favorites. As I sat across from Peter, he explained they were a small film house with projects constantly ramping up or winding down, so there would be really busy times and really slow periods in between projects. He mentioned that he had a big project coming up that was a documentary about the native american tribes of California who were going to be walking from San Diego up the whole coast of California to the capital in Sacramento to bring awareness of their tribes. He mentioned that he could use my help on that project, and once it started, we would be on the road for a few months, but things wouldn't get started for another couple of weeks. He told me to get settled into my place and get to know my way around town. He said I could call him anytime if I needed anything, but he would reach out in a few weeks to discuss our plan to start production of *The Walk*.

I was excited to set up my new studio apartment. I needed a bed, couch, fridge, and some things to make my little room my own. I drove around Hollywood checking out all of the boutique and used furniture stores. I found a decent bed, an old '70s looking rust-colored crushed velvet couch, a small fridge, and some accessories at Pier 1 Imports a short walking distance from my place. While in and out, I met a guy my age named Damien who had just moved into the house next door. He was from Flint, Michigan, and had also moved to Los Angeles to work in the film industry. From our initial discussion, we bonded over our love for hip-hop. We made plans to hang out later in the week and head out for some drinks at a place I heard about called The Room, which was walking distance. Damien stopped by at the end of the week, while I was setting up my room and listening to DJ Krush. We had a drink together at my place and then walked over to The Room.

The area was pretty rough, but it felt cool to be on the streets of Hollywood. The entrance to The Room was hidden in this little dark alley behind Cahuenga Boulevard. There was no signage, the entrance only had a red light bulb above the doorway where the bouncer stood guard. If you didn't know about the place, you would have never known it existed. It was a small bar that was dark lit with a DJ spinning records on his turntables in the back corner. It was rumored that Drew Barrymore was one of the owners. The bartender didn't care if people smoked, so we sat at the bar with our drinks, rolled a joint, lit it up, and passed it around to anyone else who wanted to join. It was an easy way to make some new friends for the night. I couldn't have been any more in love with the vibe of the place hearing the crackle of classic hip-hop vinyl bumping through the house stereo system. As we walked home that night, we talked about the DJ's set and how The Room was our new place for Thursday nights. During the walk Damien told me word on the street back in Detroit was there was an upcoming white rapper named Eminem who was making waves.

As I continued to explore the area, I found a little strip mall within walking distance on Franklin Avenue that had a swanky coffee shop called Bourgeois Pig and a rotisserie chicken place called Birds next door that became my new favorite restaurant. The strip of shops also had a liquor store with a deli and an upscale restaurant & bar. The Sunset Strip on the weekends was electric, packed with people cruising up and down in their cars or hanging out waiting to get into one of the famous hot spots. I thought the Viper Room was so cool because it was owned by Johnny Depp. The Chateau Marmot was always a cool spot to hang out if you could get in. The door guys were always trying to weed out the riff-raff, so if you didn't look the part, then they were closed for a private party that night. There always seemed to be someone famous hanging out if you looked around. As much as I loved being out on the Sunset Strip, I couldn't afford to be out all the time, so I often just hung out at my place, listening to my music or watching movies. *True Romance* was my favorite movie at the time, and it never disappointed no matter how many times I watched it. I felt like I could relate to the main character Clarence as a guy from Detroit who ventured out to Hollywood.

Peter called, and it was time to start production for *The Walk*. I met Peter at his studio so he could explain my role on the project. He said it would be just the two of us, and he could use my assistance with the camera gear and driving his Land Rover when needed while he walked with the tribes or shot footage out the window as we drove alongside them.

The night before the walk was to start, we were in San Diego for a campfire ceremony. There was a large tent on the property that Peter referred to as a sweat lodge, which I had never heard of. Peter explained we would be heading into the tent later, which would be filled with steam, designed to sweat out impurities and purify your soul. It was a unique experience to be stripped down into your underwear, sitting on the ground inside a tent that was pitch black on the inside, sweating profusely from the heat and hearing native american chants. Once the tent was closed, nobody could leave until someone broke the seal on the tent. I was just about at my breaking point when fortunately someone else beat me to the punch, exiting the tent, which ended the session. Peter and I stayed in a local hotel that night, but we were back at the campfire site early in the morning to start the walk up to Sacramento.

Over the next couple of months, Peter and I were on the road, following the tribes up the coast, capturing interviews along the way, and camping out at night with them. In the beginning, it felt like some of the tribe members didn't know what to make of us as a couple of white guys from the city following along with all of our camera gear. The further we got into the walk, the more they warmed up to us as they got to know us, and toward the end, we were treated as part of tribe.

There were points along the walk where Peter and I struggled being out in the sun all day and sleeping on the ground in a tent at night. Every now and then, we would break off from the group to get a hotel room just to take showers before camping out at night. A shower was always an appreciated luxury during that trip. One of the days when we arrived at the campsite, we noticed a water faucet with a garden hose attached. Peter and I headed to a local drug store to pick up a bar of soap and some shampoo. We took makeshift showers in our bathing suits, where one of us would hold the hose and spray, while the other would take a shower. We laughed at the whole scenario, but we slept so much better in the tent when we were clean after being out in the heat all day.

After a long couple of months, we made it to the state capital in Sacramento. There was a podium set up in a grassy area where the tribe leader Robert John and others gave speeches about the meaning and inspiration behind their walk to bring unification of the tribal nations of California. After the presentation, we said our goodbyes and thanked them for allowing us to be a part of their journey up the coast. Peter and I packed up the Land Rover and headed south down the coast back to Hollywood.

That fall, I worked in Peter's studio, learning how to log clips into the AVID editing system. I went through all of our footage from *The Walk*, breaking it down into short clips and labeling them in the system with a brief description, date, and time so each one could be easily identified later for editing. I had keys to the studio and flexible hours, so I could work whenever I wanted. I looked for other film projects where I could get more experience working on film sets. I was always looking through the classifieds in the local papers for potential opportunities. There were always projects, but the pay was little to nothing as there were so many people who wanted the experience and would work for free. It seemed film sets were always looking for grips, whose role was to provide an extra set of hands to help in setting up the lighting equipment. Working as a grip was a far cry from what I dreamed of coming to Hollywood to be a film director, but the reality had set in that it was a tough industry, and I had a lot to learn.

I looked forward to Thursday nights when Damien and I would head over to The Room. We became regulars, I loved walking down that dark alley, around the dumpsters, hearing the music filter out through the red lit doorway and walking up to the bouncer giving us a fist bump letting us stroll into the club. The Room always played hip-hop on Thursday but they brought in different DJs so it was exciting to hear their unique set each week.

Looking through Dad's bin of photo's, I came across a black & white photo I took of him holding up a couple of bundles of cash in the kitchen of the Davis Street house while I was home from Hollywood visiting him for the Christmas holidays that year. I took the photo with a Canon 35mm camera that Dad handed down to me. It was the camera he used for his photos throughout the early years of my life from late '70s to mid '80s. During my year living in Hollywood I took a photography class to work on my craft and always had Dad's old Canon with me.

I flew out of LAX and landed in Detroit late December in 1998. Dad met me at his usual spot at the bottom of the escalator in the baggage claim.

While waiting for my bag, I was caught off-guard as it looked like the actor Tom Sizemore was just standing there waiting for his bag as well. I couldn't stop staring at him, thinking it must just be someone who looked like him, and he was so casually dressed. Dad noticed my focus on him and asked why I kept staring at that guy. I told him that he was Tom Sizemore, a big-time actor who starred in *True Romance* by Tarantino.

Dad asked, "That guy in the sweat pants is a big-time movie star?!"

It was obvious to Tom that I couldn't stop looking at him, so he walked over and introduced himself. I smiled and replied "I know who you are." I told him how I recently moved to LA and was trying to break into the film industry. Tom didn't want to shatter my spirit, and looked over at Dad asking him if I was a good kid. Dad proudly replied, "He's a great kid!" and asked Tom if there was anything he could do to help me out in Los Angeles. Tom asked for my number and said he would give me a call after the holidays once both of us were back in Los Angeles. I couldn't believe the coincidence of meeting Tom Sizemore in the Detroit airport and was really hoping to hear from him after the holidays.

On the way home from the airport, Dad mentioned we needed to swing by one of his customers in the area as he had to fix one of the machines. As we walked into the bar, Dad proudly introduced me to the owner as his son who just graduated college and was now living in Los Angeles working in the movie industry. On the way back to the house, I mentioned that Jay was coming over to meet up with me as one of our old friends, Rico, was having a holiday party at his place. I was excited to see my old group of high school friends while in town.

Shortly after we got back to the house, Jay arrived. The three of us hung out in the kitchen while Dad counted out his cash on the counter from collections that day. He was putting rubber bands around fat stacks of bills for a deposit at the bank the next day when I asked him to pose for a quick picture as he smiled holding up a couple bundles of cash. I asked Dad if I could use the Cadillac while I was in town and could tell he wasn't too big on the idea. He said the Cadillac was a summer car, and he didn't take it out much in the winter.

Jay jumped into the discussion, saying, "C'mon, Dennis. When we were in Atlanta, Peter would let us take his hundred-thousand-dollar Mercedes SL 500 out. We're used to driving nice cars. It's not a big deal to us."

Dad didn't want to feel uncool, so he reluctantly allowed me to take the Cadillac but wanted the phone number for where I was going to be. Jay and I backed Dad's pristine white Eldorado out of the garage and headed to the party. I liked being back in Detroit, rolling in the Caddy with Jay in our big coats and beanies. All of our old high school buddies cheered loudly as Jay and I walked through the door and it was so good to see everyone again.

Shortly after, Dad called the house phone at the party, and Rico handed it over to me. Dad was upset, saying how uncomfortable he was with me having the Cadillac out all night. He said he wanted me to have a good time but didn't want his car out all night somewhere unknown and asked if I could bring it back. I could tell how uncomfortable he was with the situation, so I told him I would bring it back as I wasn't far away. Rico offered to follow me to Dad's house and bring me back because he wanted me to check out his new Yukon Denali. When I dropped off the keys to Dad, I told him that I was going to stay the night at Rico's since we were probably going to be up late.

We had a blast that night catching up from our early high school days together. We reminisced about that night when we had a knife pulled on us scattering off in different directions and running back to Dad's house. We drank into the early morning hours listening to music and only getting a few hours of sleep. We were back up early, congregated back in Rico's living room, recapping the night. Someone popped in Oliver Stone's *The Doors*, and we passed a bong around to help with our hangover while we watched the movie together on the couch. After the movie Jay & I headed back to Dad's house, closed the blinds and crashed on the couch to get some rest.

Just as I was about to fall asleep, I could feel Dad's presence looking over us before heading off to work for the day. He was standing in the kitchen, and asked me, "Brett, what are you gonna do today?" I knew he wanted me to help him on the route while I was home. I told him I had a late night and promised to help over the next few days if I could get some sleep. He paused and then responded with his common humorous phrase "Get busy," which meant "get to work."

I spent the next few days helping dad on the route but needed to get back to Hollywood. It wasn't like in my high school and college years where I had a long break off from school, so I felt the clock ticking and needed to get back to the grind. On the way to the airport, as we drove through the snow and slush, I joked about how I couldn't wait to get back to the sunny California weather and out of the Detroit winter. As we arrived at the airport, we got out of the van, I gave Dad a hug, and told him how much I loved him. Dad watched me walk into the airport. We had no plans to see each other again until the holidays next year. That was the last time I was in the Davis Street house with Dad.

Back in Hollywood, I was disappointed that I never heard from Tom Sizemore. Over the next few months, I continued to help Peter when needed, but since it was a small production company, there was only so much I could do. *The Walk* was now in editing, though the guy Peter had hired liked to work alone, and Peter was out looking for new projects. I continued to find these small little independent movie projects as a grip with little to no pay but continued to get more experience and was building out my network. Once on a film set, you hear about other projects the crew will be working on next, so if you had built a good relationship with them, you could ask them to help you get on the next project. I pretty much took any project that I could get onto. I even took on a student film project at Layola Marymount as they had a well-known film school. I was barely getting by financially despite Mom and Peter providing the monthly allowance for a year that was my college graduation present. I felt like the clock was ticking, and I was only a few months away from the time I would need to become financially self-sufficient.

While out for drinks with the film crew for one of the projects we had just wrapped, we were talking among ourselves at the bar. One of the producers, had asked what led me out to Hollywood. I told him I had dreams of one day making an edgy Tarantino-type of film. He wasted no time bringing me back down to reality, saying there were thousands of young guys just like me who come to LA every year with the same type of dreams that never happen. He said there was nothing unique or special about my dreams as most people in Los Angeles were chasing the same type of dream, and the number of those who actually make it was very slim. The producer's comment hit me hard, considering I was already at a point of starting to doubt my ability to succeed in Hollywood.

I went home that night really questioning myself. I had been in Hollywood almost a year with no real path to success or financial stability in sight. I only had a couple months left to figure things out. I started to think it was time to focus on finding a full-time corporate job that would provide a steady paycheck. I grew up having nice things and wanted to continue to be able to have those things in life. I liked nice clothes, I wanted to live in a nice apartment and drive a nice car. The thought of being a starving artist chasing a far-fetched dream in the movie industry was starting to seem like an unrealistic path. I was contemplating the idea of heading back to Atlanta to regroup at Mom & Peter's house while I considered my next move.

# CITY LIFE

......................

Looking through Dad's photo's, I came across the photo I thought about while in the kitchen of his house after the crime. In the photo Jay has his arm around Dad as they played cards with Jack and my Uncle Bob during a Christmas Eve party at the end of 2000. Staring at the photo, it took me back to those years after moving from Hollywood to San Francisco and those last few years for Christmas in the Riverview House.

While I was considering a move from Hollywood back to Atlanta, I reconnected with Adam, my roommate from college who was now living in San Francisco and working for a commercial real estate developer. Adam was from the Bay Area and moved back after graduating from Colorado State with a degree in Construction Management. Even before he graduated from college, Adam had his real estate license and sold a few properties in Fort Collins. We always got a good laugh out of Adam's picture on his business card—him all dressed up in a suit and tie, looking so professional and ready to sell some houses while still in college. During the call, I told Adam my thoughts around a move back to Atlanta. He told me before I moved all the way back across the country, I should visit him and check out San Francisco. A trip up the coast to check out a new city sounded like just what I needed and hit the road.

Driving into San Francisco over the Bay Bridge, I fell in love with the skyline of the city. I had never seen so many buildings packed into such a small area right on the water. Adam lived in an apartment with his girlfriend in the Marina District, which was an upscale area close to the water in between the Bay Bridge and the Golden Gate Bridge. Adam always had so much energy (overwhelming sometimes). He became such a positive influence for me during a time when I was at a crossroads and down on my situation. In the morning, we would walk down to the water before Adam had to head off to work. He was a huge cheerleader, helping to regain some confidence and was hard pressing me to move up to the city. He talked about how the city had everything I needed in such a close proximity that I could get around by walking, biking, or using public transportation and didn't even need a car. He talked about how the unemployment rate was so low, and with so much opportunity in the city, I would be able to easily find a job in no time. Before heading off to work, Adam would mention a few places for me to check out, tell me how awesome I was, and then send me off to think about what life could be like living in the city.

Walking around each day, I fell more and more in love with San Francisco. I loved the idea of living and working in the city and being able to walk to all of the local bars, restaurants, and shops. After a few days of exploring the city and all of Adam's pep talks, my mind was made up. I was ready to turn the page and move up to San Francisco. I spent the next couple of days apartment hunting and found a room for rent in a two-bedroom apartment in Pacific Heights, which was one of the nicest areas in the city.

When I met with the guy renting out the room, he introduced himself as Simon and explained that he and his girlfriend had recently broken up, so he was looking to share the place with someone else to help with the rent. I explained how I was in the process of moving from Los Angeles and planned to sell my truck to help cover the rent while I got situated with a job in the city. Simon felt confident that I would find a job quickly, so he agreed to rent the room to me. With an apartment lined up, I was ready to head back down to LA to pick up my stuff. Adam still had his same Toyota pickup truck from college and let me take it down to LA to pick up my stuff. The only things I planned to bring was my was my bed, TV, stereo, a console table (for the stereo), and clothes.

I was filled with excitement on the road trip back up to San Francisco. Upon arrival, I unloaded my stuff into my new room and returned Adam's truck to him. My new roommate Simon was a few years older, a disciplined runner and cyclist who worked in the financial services industry. Simon took me out to dinner that first night to celebrate my move into the city. It only took a few weeks to sell my truck. Knowing I had some cash to last a few months while I got situated with a new job took a little bit of pressure off.

It was shortly after, while dressed up with a stack of resumes taking a bus downtown, that a guy named Steven Smash overheard me talking on my phone about my job search, and came over to introduce himself. He went by Smash and was a tall, eccentric-looking older guy wearing a long black leather jacket, black jeans and black boots. He said he worked for a tech start-up company in the city called CarClub.com, and they were hiring sales people. He explained CarClub.com was a subscription service that provided leads to car dealers of people who were interested in their cars. Smash said, "It's a pretty easy sale as we provide free trials to the dealers for them to try out the service before committing, and we pay commission in signing up the dealers for a trial." He explained the commissions were based on the number of car lines a sales rep signed up for the service, so if you bring on an auto mall with multiple car brands, you could make some pretty good commission. He mentioned their office was pretty laid-back, and the team had a lot of fun working together.

I told him it all sounded great and asked, "How do I proceed?" Smash handed me his card with the office address and asked if I could stop by in the morning at 10:00 a.m. to meet and interview with the team. The next day, I interviewed with three people from the team, loved the vibe of the office downtown and was excited about the opportunity. I was offered the position the next day, and the compensation provided a descent base salary plus commission with full benefits.

I later became buddies with Smash and another sales rep on the team named Jonathan, who I thought looked like a better-looking version of Will Smith. Smash was a talented musician who made beats on his computer outside of work, so we were always talking about music. Jonathan rode a Hayabusa motorcycle, the fastest production bike made, to work every day wearing a black leather motorcycle jacket with Kevlar for protection. Smash and Jonathan got a kick out of me as a young clean-cut white dude who loved hip-hop.

I loved city life in San Francisco. I enjoyed riding the bus packed with people going about their daily routine to and from work every day. I liked the thrill of being in sales, knowing each day there was the potential to earn a big commission check. As I started to get the hang of sales prospecting, the commission checks started to roll in and I bought a top-of-the-line GT Zaskar mountain bike to get around. My favorite thing to do was ride around the city while listening to music through my headphones. It was very similar to how Dad loved to listen to music while roller blading around his neighborhood. I rode everywhere, and considering all of the hills in the city, I got in great shape. Every weekend, I looked forward to starting my day with a ride through the city, over the Golden Gate Bridge, and back to the apartment. There were many nights where I would ride to the middle of the Golden Gate Bridge, prop myself up against the railing, take in the view of the city lights through the fog and appreciate my new life in San Francisco.

On the weekends, I was always looking to head out to the nightclubs and check out the DJs. San Francisco had a big house music DJ scene, but I was always on the hunt for the hip-hop and trip-hop DJs. As much as I loved music, I became attracted to the idea of getting my own set of turntables. I spent some time researching, and it became clear that Technics 1200's reigned supreme.

One day after work, I took a taxi over to a stereo shop on Market Street in downtown. I asked the driver to wait for me as I would be out shortly. I walked out with two Technics 1200s turntables, a basic Gemini mixer, and loaded them into the trunk of the taxi to take back to my apartment. I had found a new obsession and loved riding my bike around the city with a messenger bag hunting for hip-hop vinyl at the local record shops. Amoeba on Haight Street was like a warehouse of vinyl and usually had whatever I was looking for. I had to have the early '90s classics in my collection but I liked finding the undiscovered underground artists that had a unique style. Digging through the crates, I came across the rap duo out of Los Angeles called People Under The Stairs and they became my favorite artists. To me they are the most underrated rap group in history. I picked up a Sony Minidisc player so I could record my own mix tapes from vinyl and listen to them on the bus to work or while riding my bike around the city.

I usually called Dad every couple of weeks to catch up and tell him what I was up to in San Francisco. During one of our calls, he mentioned that he had been dating someone new. He told me her name was Rachel, and she was a much younger girl who was a cocktail waitress at one of the hottest nightclubs in the area. It sounded like things had gotten pretty serious as he mentioned she had been staying at the house. Dad told me that Rachel had a young daughter named Alison, and he had been thinking about getting a bigger house that would provide more space for the three of them. Shortly after, Dad sold the Davis Street house in Wyandotte and bought a new house in Riverview in the same neighborhood we had lived as a family before my parents' divorce. The new house was a big upgrade from the Davis Street house as a four-bedroom two-story house with a large finished basement. Considering the growth of Dad's business, the new house also provided a much larger garage space to store CDs, cigarettes, vending machines and parts.

Just before the holidays that year, Peter Jr. called with some exciting news. He told me that his film *The Walk* was accepted into the 2000 Sundance Film Festival in Park City, UT in January and wanted me to join him. Sundance was the largest independent film festival in the country. This was quite the accomplishment as many filmmakers go their whole career and never make it into Sundance. When I shared the news with Jay, it turned out he was also planning to head to Sundance as the start-up media company he was working for, called Zoom Culture, was attending the event.

I made plans to head back to Detroit to spend a week with Dad for Christmas before heading to Utah in January. I flew out of SFO and landed back in Detroit. I was excited to see Dad's new house. He met me at his usual spot at the bottom of the escalator by the baggage claim. We picked up my bag, jumped in the van, and made our way back to the house. When we arrived at the house, Rachel was waiting for us in the kitchen. My immediate thought was that she was definitely Dad's type as a pretty petite blonde.

The three of us had a drink in the kitchen while Rachel and I got to know each other a bit. I was surprised to find out she was only five years older than me and had attended the same high school I went to in Riverview. Rachel had graduated one year before I started my freshman year. I arrived late and was tired from my travels so we called it an early night.

I woke up in the morning on the living room couch, opening my eyes to Dad wearing his drugstore readers, and checking his stocks in the paper over coffee before he heading off to work. As I sat up on the couch to say good morning, he mentioned he could use my help while in town but didn't need me for anything that day. He told me to relax with Rachel at the house, and he wanted to take us out later that evening to show me some of the new hot spots. I asked if I could bring Jay as I was excited to see him while in town. Shortly after Dad headed out the door, Rachel came downstairs in a robe and asked if I wanted to smoke with her. It seemed part of her normal morning routine, and suggested we smoke out in the garage.

After we walked into the garage, I took a seat on box filled with cartons of cigarettes, and we lit up a joint. I looked around the garage, which had all of the vending products on one side and Dad's white Cadillac Eldorado parked on the other side. The far side wall in the garage had these tall and narrow windows that were tinted on the outside so you could see out but couldn't see into the garage. I loved Dad's Eldorado as it reminded me of him so much. I couldn't believe it was an early '90s model but still looked brand-new. As we talked about the Eldorado, Rachel mentioned how it barely had any miles on it. She said Dad didn't drive it much, only taking it out on special occasions.

With Rachel being so young, I really wanted to feel her out about her feelings toward Dad. Through our discussions, I got the sense that she really liked him. She talked about how well Dad treated her and took good care of her. After we finished the joint, we headed back into the house as it was cold in the garage. As we walked through the door, I looked back at the Caddy in the garage. The exact spot where I was sitting on the box of cigarettes is where Dad was found after the crime just over eight years later.

I spent the morning checking out Dad's new house. The outside of the house was a light brown stucco, and the interior was completely white. It was a tri-level house with a main front door and then a side entrance right next to the garage doors. The garage had another separate entrance around the other side of the house. The main level had two large living rooms connected by a little kitchen in between. In the main living room, Dad had a large sofa and big-screen TV. The other large living room was empty as he had so much more space than our little house on Davis street, and the house had yet to be fully furnished. He had a picture of me from high school framed on a console table behind the couch in the main room. The main living room had a sliding glass door that opened to a small deck area where he had a grill set up. Above the deck was a little balcony off one of the upstairs bedrooms. Downstairs was a large finished basement with a bar and a jacuzzi room. Upstairs were four bedrooms and two bathrooms, which included the master suite, two bedrooms and then another room Dad used as an office.

Later that afternoon, Dad arrived back at the house. He mentioned he wanted to take us out to a nice dinner and then check out a few bars that he wanted me to see while in town. I told Dad that I had invited Jay to join us. When Jay arrived, we all had a drink together in the kitchen, then piled into the Cadillac for a night out on the town. After dinner, Dad was excited to show me this new hot spot called Clutch Cargo's, which was formerly a church that had been converted into a nightclub. The place was completely packed and quite a scene. Hip-hop music filled the venue. Dad headed to the bar to get drinks.

While we hung out with Rachel, this younger good-looking guy approached Rachel to try and pick her up. At first, Jay and I were calm as it came about unexpectedly, but the longer the guy kept talking to her, the more annoyed by the situation we became. Rachel enjoyed the attention. Dad made his way back to us and was unfazed by the situation, handing Rachel her drink. The guy looked Dad up and down, probably thinking he was a much better catch than Dad, who was so much older, and so he kept talking to Rachel. At that point, Jay had enough, asking why he was still here when it was clear Rachel was with my dad. The guy stood there for a second then backed off and walked away. Jay looked over at Dad to find him completely calm. Jay asked Dad if that bothered him, and he responded by saying no, he was flattered by the fact a young good-looking guy was interested in his girlfriend. Dad seemed to be completely confident in the scenario.

After the Christmas holiday, I spent a few days helping Dad out on the vending route. We drove from bar to bar, collecting cash, replenishing the machines, and fixing any issues. During the drives between bars, we talked about Dad starting a new chapter in his life with the new house and taking care of Rachel and her daughter Alison, who would be moving in. It was a quick visit that year as I had plans to celebrate New Year's with friends in Lake Tahoe. Dad drove me to the airport, and we said our goodbyes as I made my way back to San Francisco.

A few weeks into the New Year, it was time to head to the Sundance Film Festival in Park City. It was the first time I had ever been to Park City, and I absolutely loved the ski town. It was like Hollywood took over the town for that week. I was so excited to have a film that I had worked on with Peter in the festival. I met up with Jay as soon as I arrived in town, we were both excited to go to as many of the parties as possible. We barhopped around town and were invited to a couple of local house parties. Jay was always good at finding the after-parties keeping us out into the early morning hours.

At the premiere of *The Walk*, it was so fun to see the final cut on the big screen and relive everything that went into making the film with Peter that summer. Even though I was only an assistant on the film, it was still rewarding to have been a part of a project that was accepted into Sundance.

# DAD, JACK & THE CADILLAC

....................

At the end of 2000, I made my usual plans to head back to Detroit to spend a week with Dad over Christmas. On the drive back to the house, Dad mentioned Jack had recently moved into one of the upstairs bedrooms. Dad said that he and Rachel had broken up but still saw each other from time to time. He mentioned that someone had broken into his house a little while back while he was out. After the incident, he felt uncomfortable living alone, so he asked Jack to move in since he was also working with Dad, helping with the vending business. Dad mentioned that whoever broke into the house got into his safe and took some cash, jewelry, and his Red Wings hockey tickets. I couldn't help to think it was funny that they took his Red Wings tickets. I told Dad he should show up at the game, go to his seats, and would probably find the robbers sitting there wearing all his shit. We laughed as we pulled into the driveway.

As we walked into the house, Jack was in the kitchen waiting for us. Jack was like family and had always been around our family. We had a drink together in the kitchen, catching up on the latest in my life living in San Francisco. Dad mentioned we had plans in a few hours to drop off holiday gift baskets to some of his customers and wanted to take the Caddy out. After getting cleaned up, the three of us met back in the kitchen, ready to head out.

Walking into the garage that year, I noticed it was much more organized than when I was there the previous year. Dad showed me everything he had done to the garage. He had installed shelving along the wall for his products & parts and built a loft space overhead for additional storage. He showed me a large safe that he had mounted against the wall next to the door that provided direct access to the side of the house next to his neighbor. Leaning up against the wall next to the door was my 1987 Haro Freestyle bike. I loved that bike and told Dad that I couldn't believe he still had it. He said he thought it was a cool bike and could be worth a lot of money someday. The white Eldorado still looked like it hadn't been driven, and I was excited that we were taking it out that night. I jumped in the backseat with Jack riding shotgun.

Dad was a huge Rod Stewart fan, so we listened to his greatest hits album as we drove from bar to bar, dropping off gift baskets and spending time with Dad's customers. Sitting in the backseat, it was funny listening to Dad & Jack's back and forth banter with each other. It reminded me of the same type of relationship I had with my roommates in college. It was always fun to be out at the downriver bars during the holidays seeing everyone in the holiday spirit keeping warm from the blistering cold with the streets covered in snow. The scene was the same every bar we walked into. Dad led, holding the gift basket, then Jack, and I trailed behind. I was wearing a black fur lined charcoal grey car coat that I bought for my trip back to Detroit. As we walked through the door, the regulars would scream out, "Dennis...Jack!" excited to see them. Dad would set the basket on the bar and order a round of drinks for everyone. Dad & Jack were the life of the party, and everyone loved them. Dad was always proud, introducing me to his customers, friends, and the pretty cocktail waitresses. I had so much fun that night hanging out with Dad & Jack, playing games on Dad's machines and loading up music on the jukeboxes. That night was my favorite memory being out on the town with Dad & Jack. I loved seeing them in their element.

That year, Dad & Jack hosted the Langley family Christmas party at the Riverview House. Jay was back in town for the holidays from Los Angeles, so I invited him over. My grandma and Aunt Cathy cooked a big feast for everyone, and after dinner, everyone got together to play the card game called Screw Your Neighbor. Everyone was having a blast celebrating the holidays together. As the night went on, people started filtering out, and the night ended with Dad, Jack, Jay, and my Uncle Bob continuing to play cards in the kitchen. They had upped the stakes on their bets and were having a great time.

I took a couple steps back and found the right angle capturing the photo of them playing with Jay's arm around Dad. It is one of my favorite photos from that time period.

After Christmas, I spent a few days driving around with Dad, helping out on the vending route. I asked about the breakup with Rachel. He mentioned she was a lot to deal with and was on a lot of medication to keep her mentally stable. Dad mentioned that even though Rachel was seeing someone else, he still helped her financially. I asked why he felt the need to do that if she was seeing someone else. He said even though they weren't together, he still cared about her and didn't like to see her struggle.

When I asked how things were with work, he said things were going really well, but it was a tough business. He mentioned that a large portion of his business was based on the poker machines. He told me that for regular customers, they would pay out as if it were like playing a real game in Vegas, which drew in a lot of business. Gambling wasn't legal at the time in Detroit so this was only with regular trusted customers. I was worried about him being involved in that piece of his business. He told me it was a huge portion of his business, and if he didn't have it, then he would lose a lot of his accounts to competitors who would provide the service. Dad mentioned how he was worried that a lot of people knew he ran a cash-based business, and that was the reason behind upgrading the safe at the house in the garage. Dad said he had a hard time hiring anyone else besides Jack because it was hard to trust anyone dealing with an all-cash business.

Dad told me I always had the option to come home to Detroit and take over the business since he trusted me more than anyone. He told me I could make a lot of money and the business could provide a great life living in Michigan. I really appreciated Dad's offer and his trust in me, but I told him I wanted to find my own path and liked living in California. Dad told me the option was always there for me, and whatever I do, "Just go, go, go." I asked if he was saving money toward retirement. He kind of chuckled and said his money was tied up in the business. He said he would work until he died and planned to run the business for many years to come. In Dad's mind, the idea of being old or retired was a long ways away. He told me whenever he did pass away, the business would be mine and worth a lot of money.

Just before New Year's, Dad dropped me off at the airport. I gave him a hug and told him how great it was to see him over the holidays. Dad saw me off as I walked through the front doors of the Detroit airport. That was the last time I was in Detroit, until I returned after what happened the night of February 27th in 2008 at Dad's house.

# THE ESTATE

·················

In the months following the crime, I was talking with my estate lawyer on a regular basis, trying to make progress on how to handle Dad's house and the business. I hired a company to go through Dad's house to document everything of value to maximize the insurance claim. Since I wasn't able to be back in Detroit on a full-time basis and wasn't familiar with the process of filing the claim, it worked out well to have someone take ownership. Dad's '92 Cadillac Eldorado ended up being worth quite a bit considering the year and unusually low milage. For Dad's business, Jimmy was servicing the accounts while we continued to build out a spreadsheet of all of the accounts and inventory. After a couple of months of collections, we weren't seeing revenues anywhere near what Dad had reported on his last couple years of tax returns.

I planned a short trip back to Detroit to meet with my estate lawyer and discuss the latest progress on the estate. When I arrived in Detroit, my Uncle Dave picked me up from the airport. I planned to stay with he and Aunt Mickey while in town. The next morning, I headed over to my estate lawyer's office. We had everything finalized for the insurance claim on the house and I wanted to determine the best way to proceed. Considering we had maxed out the insurance claim, determined what was owed on the mortgage and had estimated costs to rebuild Dad's house the numbers just weren't adding up to rebuild the house. Detroit had been hit extremely hard by the financial crisis of 2008, and every month, real estate values plunged deeper and deeper. Dad had taken out a loan against the house shortly before the crime, but we were unable to determine what the funds were used for. We assumed that the money was used to invest in bar renovations for one of his new Valu Vending customers, but without any documentation, we were not able to determine where the money went, and nobody was owning up to it. All things considered, the only option was to demolish the house and sell off the land.

During this time, I had been contacted by an entertainment company that Dad had signed a contract with shortly before he passed away to pay multiple years of royalties for the use of their particular poker game that they owned the rights to. In reviewing the contract and the amount owed on a monthly basis, there was no way we would be able to cover the royalties considering current revenues. We decided to try and cut ties with the poker game company. Jimmy removed the computer chips in the tabletop poker machines and we shipped them back to the entertainment company with a legal letter explaining that with the dramatic change in the business we were not able to meet the terms of the royalty agreement put in place when Dad was running the business.

Valu Vending had been in a constant decline with Dad's customers moving to his competitors because of the incentives they were providing to make the switch. Without Dad in the picture, his customers were ready to move on and probably felt they were off the hook on any money owed to Valu Vending without a contract in place. It felt like we were on a sinking boat and couldn't scoop buckets of water out fast enough to keep things afloat. All we could do is try to keep as many customers as possible, collect whatever we could, and complete our documentation of all assets and revenue for the potential to sell off the business as quickly as possible. The whole scenario was a complete nightmare as I tried to determine any kind of a positive path forward. Dad was gone, there was nothing that could be done to bring him back, we were still in the dark with the police as to exactly what happened, and I was left trying to pick up the pieces. There wasn't much else I could do while in town, so I had Uncle Dave drop me off at the airport so I could head home to my life back in Orange County.

# DAVIS HOUSE DREAM

. . . . . . . . . . . . . . . . . . .

I was always looking for signs from Dad that he was in a better place. The song "Rocket Man" kept coming on in the most random places, which would give me goosebumps because it felt like it was Dad's way of letting me know he was with me. One night, I had a dream where I truly felt his presence. In my dream, I was back in the Davis Street House. I was anxiously pacing around the kitchen, checking my watch and waiting for him to come home. Shortly after, I watched him stroll by the window that was over the sink facing the driveway as he made his way to the side door. As he walked through the door, I felt a sense of relief that he was ok and gave him a big hug.

In the dream, we didn't talk about the details of what took place in the Riverview house the night of the murders, but it felt that we were both aware of what had happened. Dad seemed happy and proceeded to tell me that he was ok and in a good place now. He told me to move on with my life, and he would always be with me. He told me to not let the situation of what happened bring me down too much and to enjoy every minute I could with my family because you never know what could happen in life. He told me that he was proud of me and the life I had built with my beautiful family. The dream was short, but when I woke up I felt an overwhelming sense of peace. As I laid in bed processing the dream looking at the ceiling, I took comfort in the fact that when Dad passed away, he knew how much I loved him and vice versa.

# BIRTHDAY BOY

· · · · · · · · · · · · · · · · · · ·

It was July 22, 2008, and our boy's first Birthday. We had been in our Canoe Pond house for about eight months and were looking forward to having family and friends over to celebrate with us. Jennifer went all out decorating our garage so we could make the best use of space in our little house. My mom & Peter flew into town along with Jenn's parents for the special day. We invited our friends and neighbors to join us. It was a gorgeous summer day at the house. Everyone congregated in the garage around Jake in his high chair as we sang "Happy Birthday." He was in good spirits and seemed to enjoy all of the attention.

The whole scenario reminded me of my third birthday party that Dad had recorded at the house on his VHS camera with everyone singing to me. I thought about how much easier it was for us to document these special moments on our phones compared to Dad capturing my early birthdays on a big VHS camera and taking photos on his late '70s Canon 35mm camera that he handed down to me. We also had social media which made it easier to keep a timeline of special moments over the years. I kept thinking about how Dad was thirty-two when I turned one and now I was thirty-two for Jake's first Birthday. For the rest of my life, I would continue to think about special moments with Jake and how it was probably similar for Dad with me, considering the exact same age difference between father and son.

# DNA RESULTS

.....................

It was early December of 2008, when the Riverview police called to let me know they had the DNA results from Dad's house. The detective proceeded to tell me there wasn't any DNA matching the three teenagers that they had in custody, but there had been a match with a forty-one-year-old guy named Doyle Palmer. I wasn't sure how to process the news as I thought the police were confident they had those involved with the teenagers the past nine months. By this time I was expecting that we were heading to trial soon to prosecute the teenagers, hear the details of what had happened at Dad's house and bring some sort of justice to the whole situation.

The detective told me that since Alison's confession had no mention of Doyle Palmer and they did not find any DNA at the house matching the teenagers, the teenagers had been released and Doyle Palmer was taken into custody. Confused, I asked about Alison's confession, and the detective told me that they had no documentation of the confession as the police station used in the interrogation was an older facility without any recording equipment. It had turned out that they had brought Doyle Palmer in for questioning days after the crime, and even though he had a black eye and a severe cut on his arm, they let him go when he related the injuries to a recent bar fight. He had also been convicted of a similar arson charge previously. The police were so focused on the teenagers as the ones responsible, that they overlooked Doyle's questioning immediately after the crime.

When I asked if we would be going to trial right away based on these latest developments, I was told that, considering the change in suspects and the direction of the case, it would take some time and the clock determining a trial date would start over. The detective told me they couldn't provide more detail as it was an active investigation and everything would need to come out in court as part of the trial.

After the discussion with the detective, my family and I were left completely confused. Everything we had thought for the last nine months about what had happened in Dad's house was thrown out the window. I had no idea who Doyle Palmer was and had never heard any mention of him over the years. Talking over the situation with my family, nobody knew him. The only link we had was that Doyle Palmer was close friends with Jeff Peterson, the guy I had driven around to Dad's customers with Jimmy Martin, weeks after the crime. Doyle and Jeff lived in the same trailer park together. There was mention that Dad's ex-girlfriend Rachel may have known Doyle and Jeff, but we didn't know that for sure.

We were all convinced that this wasn't a one-man job with Doyle acting alone. How could one man kill two people, take a large safe from the house, set Dad's van on fire blocks from the crime scene, and leave the area all by himself? Even though I still felt the teenagers were involved, where there's smoke there's fire, it seemed strange to me that the teenagers would be involved with a forty-one year old guy to carry out the crime. So the only concrete evidence we had was DNA from a random guy named Doyle Palmer who was in Dad's house the night of the murders. We would now need to continue and wait for the new trial date to get the details.

# BUST

·····················

At the beginning of 2009, my estate lawyer called to let me know that a lawsuit had been filed against me and the estate, from the entertainment company that Dad had signed the multiyear royalty agreement with in order to use their particular poker game in his machines. They were not going to accept us returning the computer chips from the tabletop poker machines and cancelling the agreement. Even though Valu Vending's revenues were a fraction of what they once were and we were not able to cover the royalties, the company felt they had a strong legal case for the money owed as part of the multiyear agreement. I was in complete shock that anybody had the heart to sue me along with the estate considering what had happened to Dad. It was a reminder of the type of people we were dealing with in the industry. My estate lawyer recommended we bring in another lawyer who specialized in similar types of cases as it was outside of his expertise to review the details of the lawsuit and recommend our course of action. My estate lawyer said the lawsuit required a response within a short period of time and couldn't be delayed or ignored.

# VISITING GRANDMA

....................

A few days later, my estate lawyer called back and sounded excited about something. He proceeded to tell me that he wasn't sure how it was overlooked in the process, but he had found a small life insurance policy that Dad had put in place from 1991 with Grandma as the beneficiary. He asked if I was close with my grandma and if I would be able to talk to her about how she would like the proceeds to be handled. I told him I did have a good relationship with her, would schedule a trip back to Detroit right away to discuss the situation with her and we could also meet to discuss the latest in the lawsuit against me and the estate.

I called Grandma to see if I could come visit her as part of my trip back to Detroit. Grandma lived alone in an assisted living apartment as my grandpa had passed away years earlier. I caught a flight back to Detroit within days and stopped by Grandma's place. When we sat down, I told her I wanted to talk to her about something related to Dad. I don't think she had fully grasped what had happened to him, and I thought that was probably a good thing. After Dad & Jack passed away, Grandma told Aunt Cathy, during one of her visits, that Dad & Jack had just come to visit her in her apartment. I really like to believe that visit did happen in some shape or form. Before Grandma had moved into the assisted living home, there were a couple of years where she had lived with Dad & Jack at the Riverview house. Dad had set up the whole second large living area downstairs off of the kitchen as her own living space. I always got a kick out of thinking about the three of them living together and their dynamic as roommates. Grandma loved to cook for Dad & Jack at night. Grandma would get mad at Jack, mentioning he would always drink her Vernors pop coming home late at night.

I proceeded to tell her that Dad had set up a life insurance policy going back to 1991 and she was the beneficiary. I asked how she would like to handle it as part of Dad's estate. Grandma told me that he was my dad, and since I was his only child, she felt the money should go to me. After being sure that she understood the scenario and that was what she wanted to do, I told her that she would need to sign some paperwork and the estate lawyer would put it together for her to review as part of the closing of the estate.

I loved my grandma, and we had such a great relationship over the years. She always made me feel like I was a special kid in the family. It made me think of a memory when I lived with Dad in the Davis Street house during my early years of high school. One day, she was triggered by looking through one of the local department store catalogues, and decided to get in the car to head over to Dad's house. She pulled in the driveway, and we watched her walking up the driveway to the side door with this catalogue in her hand. Dad met her at the door and let her inside. She was on a mission, telling Dad that he really needed to get me into modeling. She showed him the pictures of the boys my age in the catalogue, saying that I was even better looking. Dad chuckled at the whole situation and looked over at me to see if I was getting as big of a kick out of the discussion as he was. I smiled at Dad and put my hands up like it was something for him to handle on his own. It was like I wasn't even there; she just wanted to make her point to Dad, like he needed to realize that he was overlooking something. To appease her, Dad agreed that I was a good-looking kid and would look into it as she walked back to her car to drive back to her house down the street.

After my visit with Grandma, I headed over to my estate lawyer's office as he had lined up another lawyer to review the lawsuit and determine our best course of action. Upon review, it was recommended that we not fight the lawsuit as we would burn through a lot of money in lawyer fees and he didn't anticipate a positive outcome. He said unfortunately the best course of action would be to comply by turning Valu Vending and all of the associated assets over to the entertainment company filing the lawsuit. I couldn't believe that I would be turning over what was left of the business that Dad had worked for so many years building up. I thought about my dream with Dad at the Davis street house and him telling me to move on with my life. The business had died off with Dad when he passed away. I signed the paperwork, and Valu Vending was no longer in business.

# THE CHAS BAR

··················

The Chas Bar was a small bar in Wyandotte by the train tracks that was owned by my Uncle Chuck and Aunt Nancy. Their son Jeff, who was my cousin, ran the day-to-day operations, working behind the bar. Everyone loved Jeff and enjoyed having him as their bartender. It was our local place where my family went on a regular basis for events, celebrations, holidays, or just a fun night out, drinking and listening to music on the jukebox. Chas Bar was a long-time customer of Valu Vending. It was the last place Dad & Jack were seen before heading back to the house the night of the crime. They usually went to the Chas Bar on Wednesday nights after bowling to wind down the night. The night of the crime, Jack headed back to the house earlier than usual, Dad following him about an hour later. In talking with family and friends who were with Dad & Jack that night, they said they were in good spirits, and it was one of their more mellow nights. It was just a usual Wednesday night, and nobody could have expected what was about to unfold when Dad & Jack had walked out the door of Chas Bar that night.

Aunt Nancy and Jeff knew what was going on with the lawsuit and called me regularly to see how things were coming along. After the decision had been made to turn over Valu Vending to the new company, I told them the scenario. I explained there was nothing I could legally do; based on the royalty agreement Dad had signed, I was on the hook to their company for more than we were seeing with the current revenues of Valu Vending. I told them I had turned over all of the assets of Valu Vending, and the new company would be taking over collections and servicing of the machines. They asked if I got anything out of the deal, and I told them that I got nothing as part of the takeover.

A few days later, a guy from the new vending company, who would be servicing Dad's machines moving forward came into Chas Bar. Aunt Nancy was waiting and gave him a piece of her mind. She told the guy that unless they worked out something with me, giving me a portion of the collections from Chas Bar, they would no longer be a customer. Aunt Nancy told them Chas Bar was a family owned business and I was family. She told him that she couldn't believe, after everything that had happened, they had the nerve to just stroll into Chas Bar to service Dad's machines like they were their own. The guy tried to explain that he wasn't part of the decisions made at the company and was just there to service the machines on behalf of the company. He said he would discuss the situation with his company and figure out a path forward.

I got a call within days to discuss a potential deal that would allow the new vending company to keep Chas Bar as a customer with me getting a fair amount as a monthly check. We agreed to $500 a month as a royalty as long as I helped to keep things in good standing with Chas Bar. I spoke with Aunt Nancy and Jeff and told them I was happy with the agreement, considering I had accepted there was nothing for me in the turnover of Valu Vending.

I was so grateful to my Aunt Nancy, Uncle Chuck, and Jeff for stepping in. It felt like the only positive thing that had come out of the situation. I told them that I was going to use the $500 a month toward Jake's preschool as Dad would have liked that. Jeff called me on a regular basis each month after the deal was in place to be sure that I had received my monthly check.

# VIRTUAL MEMORIAL TOAST

......................

The evening of February 27th, 2009, one year exactly from the night when everything had happened at Dad's house, Uncle Dave called to tell me a group of family and friends were heading down to Chas Bar later that night to do a toast for Dad & Jack, and asked me to join over FaceTime. Later that night at about 11:00 p.m. EST, which was the time we all anticipated that everything had happened at Dad's house, Uncle Dave called me for the toast.

I poured myself a whiskey on the rocks and went over to the black marble urn on the bookcase next to our TV in the living room. Uncle Dave kicked off the toast, saying, "Here's to Dennis & Jack," as I held my glass up to everyone with the black marble urn visible in my video next to me. It was an emotional moment with everyone tearing up as we thought about the situation and the fact that exactly one year ago they were with Dad & Jack in The Chas Bar just like any other night before what happened. Even though it had been a year, we still didn't have closure as to what had happened in Dad's house that night which dramatically changed our lives forever.

# FIVE-YEAR ANNIVERSARY

·····················

On February 28th, 2009, Jenn and I celebrated our five-year anniversary. We found a babysitter to watch Jake, so we could head out for a nice dinner together to celebrate. Sitting across from her, I kept thinking about how much in love with her I was. She was not only drop-dead gorgeous, but I had seen a new side to her becoming such an amazing mother. She had been my rock the past year as I went through the toughest year of my life, always being so supportive and a burst of sunshine during many dark moments. Everything in life had been pretty easy up until 2008, without her by my side and Jake in our life, I don't know if I would have made it through.

I have this memory from that year that always puts me at ease. I was walking by the upstairs bathroom outside of Jake's room and caught her singing to Jake while she bathed him. The sun was lined up perfectly shining down on him through the little window in the shower. She had her back to me and didn't see me walking by as I stopped in the doorway to appreciate the moment. She seemed so happy just being a mother and singing like no one was around. It was such a beautiful and peaceful moment that is stuck in my mind. It was moments like that that made me feel better days were ahead after such a tough year. Later that night as we got into bed, I closed my eyes and my mind took me back to when we reconnected after college leading up to the present.

# BACK IN TOUCH

...................

In early 2001, I had reconnected with a younger guy named Jake, who was in our fraternity, and moved to the Bay Area after college with his girlfriend, Ann. Jake & Ann lived about thirty minutes south of San Francisco in a town called Mountain View. Jake was into vinyl, had a set of turntables, and played house music. Jake and I immediately bonded over our love for music and playing on the turntables. Jake & Ann would come up to the city on the weekends to stay with me while we would head out to the nightclubs. They wanted to move into the city, so we decided to look for a two-bedroom apartment together splitting the rent three ways, lowering each of our monthly rents since it was so expensive to live in the city. Considering Jake & Ann worked in Mountain View, we decided it made sense to look at places in the southern part of the city, which would be central for all of our commutes. We focused on the Sunset area as rents were much more reasonable than living close to downtown.

Considering a lower monthly rent and moving more to the outskirts of the city, I decided it was time for me to get another car. I loved Mitsubishi Montero Sports, which were a bigger, nicer version of the Trooper that I had last. After hunting online for a few weeks, I found a perfect used white Montero Sport LS in Los Angeles and negotiated the best price possible. Once the deal was locked, I bought a one-way flight down to Los Angeles, took a taxi to the dealership, strolled into the showroom excited to pick up my new truck, and drove it back up to San Francisco. It was great to be back on the road again, and I absolutely loved my new Montero.

It was shortly after that I got word that CarClub.com was going out of business. I enjoyed my time working at CarClub, but I always wondered how the company made money paying salespeople commission on deals that didn't have guaranteed revenue after the trial period. It just didn't seem like a sustainable business model. Now that I had a car, I was able to open up my job search to a larger radius outside of the city and now had some sales experience. It didn't take long for me to find another tech sales job. I accepted an offer with a large data center company who had an office about an hour outside of the city. I didn't mind the commute, as I loved driving the Montero, and it seemed like a great opportunity. Once Jake, Ann, and I were situated in our new place together, we continued our routine of work during the week, spending the weekends at the local summer street festivals during the day and then heading out to the nightclubs at night. The three of us were enjoying city life and did everything together.

I had been thinking about my ex-girlfriend Jennifer from college and was curious where she ended up after graduation. I put the word out to my friends who had moved to Denver after college that I wanted to try and get back in touch with her. I asked them to get her number if they happen to run into her. Sure enough, about a month later, one of my friends ran into Jennifer, mentioned I was trying to reach her, got her number, and passed it onto me. I called the number immediately and got the answering machine at Jennifer's parents' house. I left a voicemail with her parents, saying I was an old friend from college who was trying to reach Jennifer and left my number.

It was a few days later while I was at a summer street festival in the city when Jennifer called. I got excited when I saw the Denver area code and hoped it was her. I answered, it was so great to hear Jennifer's voice again and she was excited to hear from me. It was loud at the festival, so I quickly made my way to a quieter place. I was in the Marina District on Union Street, so I walked up to the top of Fillmore and Broadway, which had a great view of the bay. I took a seat on the steps at the top of Fillmore Street and couldn't believe that I was actually on the phone with Jennifer. I told her about my life the past three years since leaving Fort Collins, spending a year in Hollywood before moving up to San Francisco. She told me that she had gotten engaged to a guy after college and had moved to San Diego, but backed out of the engagement and moved back to Denver. She was living with her parents until she could find her own place and was working at a furniture & artwork store in the city called Z Gallerie. We talked for an hour and I was so happy to be back in touch with her.

That fall, a group of friends from Colorado State had coordinated a get-together for a CSU football game that was in Denver. I probably wouldn't have gone if it was just for a football game but wanted to go for the potential to see Jennifer while in town. At this point, we were in regular contact over the phone and through email. When I brought it up to her on one of our regular calls, she said she wasn't able to attend the game as she had to work that day, but we scheduled some time to meet for lunch the following day while I was in town.

We made plans to meet for lunch at a local Mexican restaurant that Jennifer liked by her work. As I waited for her out front, she came walking down the street and was still as gorgeous as ever. As we talked over lunch, she seemed really happy with her life in Denver. We always had such a strong chemistry between us, and it seemed as we still both liked each other very much. However, considering how far apart we were from each other, we had to settle for a long-distance friendship. After lunch, Jenn and I said our goodbyes. We kissed, and I told her how happy I was to be back in touch, always looking forward to our calls and email exchanges.

It was early morning September 11, 2001, when I woke up to Jake & Ann calling for me to come see what was going on. As I walked into our living room still half asleep, I didn't understand what they were watching. One of the Twin Towers in New York had smoke billowing out of the gaping hole in the side, and I asked them if it was a movie. They said that a plane had flown into the side of one of the towers, and shortly after, we watched the second plane crash into the other tower in real time. Once the magnitude of what was happening sunk in, I had the scary realization that our country was under attack.

The news said we were on a lockdown until they could figure out the situation, and homeland security was working to avoid potential for other attacks. The news mentioned that our major bridges were potential targets. I wasn't sure what to do as I drove over the Bay Bridge for work every day. I hadn't seen anything about our office being closed, so I decided that I should head to work as usual. On the drive, I called my manager to ask if the office was closed. She had not seen the news and was unaware of what had happened. As I explained the situation, she wasn't sure what to say, so I continued with my usual commute. Upon arriving at the office, I found everyone had heard the news by now and was glued to their devices to hear the latest. The office ended up closing over the next few days.

I had heard again the mention of the Bay Bridge being a potential target and became worried about my commute back and forth once the office had opened back up. After a few days of considering the potential of staying at a friend's house who lived on the other side of the bridge, I decided I wasn't going to alter my life based on fear as that was what terrorists strived for. Once the office opened back up, I continued with my normal commute. On the drive home one day, I called Dad. When Dad answered, I was driving across the Bay Bridge. The first thing he said was that he hoped I wasn't driving across the bridges in San Francisco. I told him I was on the Bay Bridge as we spoke. At that very moment, an ambulance drove by with loud sirens. Dad became very worried, asking me if I was crazy for driving on the bridge with everything going on. I told him I didn't want to live my life in fear.

I said, "When it's my time, it will be my time, and it's probably unavoidable." We talked about the whole situation the country was going through, and I told him how much I loved him.

It was in the spring of 2002 when my roommates Jake & Ann were going through a rough patch in their relationship and decided they were going to split up once our lease came due for renewal. A few months before our lease was up for renewal, I was laid off from my company due to a large reduction in workforce. The tech industry as a whole was going through a tough period after the dot-com bust. Fortunately, I had closed a large deal before the layoff, which provided my biggest commission check to date. Considering the commission check along with severance pay, I was in good shape financially to take some time to determine my next step.

Considering how expensive rent was in San Francisco and with the Bay Area tech industry in such a rough place, I decided I wanted to move back down to sunny Southern California. I had Jay, who now lived in Los Angeles; a group of college friends who had moved to Hermosa Beach; and Adam, who was further south, living in Newport Beach. I had two months left on my lease, and Jake's younger brother wanted to move into the city, so he took over my rent for those remaining months.

Jay offered to let me stay with him for as long as needed. Jay lived in a large house in Glendale, renting one of the large bedrooms. The evening I planned to arrive, Jay was hosting a film premiere party for one of his projects at a swanky bar in Hollywood and asked if I wanted to DJ the event. I hit the road down to Southern California with just my turntables, records and clothes. I arrived at Jay's place, and we caught up over a few drinks before his event. I had a blast DJing at Jay's film premiere. I felt my set was perfect, and it was fun to be hosting an event with Jay upon my arrival back to Southern California.

I made my rounds in Southern California, enjoying some time off to determine where I wanted to settle down next. I made plans to spend some time with one of my college buddies Mark, who was living in a beach front condo in Hermosa Beach. Mark urged me to enjoy the summer and not rush into a new job right away, offering up his couch for me to stay. Mark was a good-looking guy, who was well off, drove a Land Rover Defender 90, and was known by the local beach bars staff & regulars. There were a few other guys from our fraternity who had also moved to Hermosa Beach. They had become close with a group of pretty girls who were always around. There was always a group relaxing at the beach, heading to a house party, or hanging out at the local beach bars. Hermosa Beach was like a never-ending beach party utopia with anything you wanted.

After spending a couple weeks in Hermosa, I was ready to start looking into finding my own place and winding things down. I felt living in Hermosa full-time would make it very difficult to focus on work during the week. I also didn't want to move back to the hustle and bustle of Hollywood, so I put my focus on Orange County. I felt like it was the smartest choice, and with Hermosa and Hollywood being only an hour drive away, I could always go up on the weekends to have some fun. I made my way down to Newport Beach to stay with Adam while I started my search for an apartment and a new job.

Adam had recently sold his first condo in Newport Beach after a remodel and flipping it for a good profit. He was now living in his second property, which had three units, and was walking distance to "The Wedge", a well-known surf spot. He lived in one of the units and rented out the other two. At the time, he had a side hustle flipping Ferraris. One of his tenants worked at the local Ferrari dealership and asked Adam to partner with him in buying out reservations from people who decided to back out on their rare Ferrari orders. They would then sell the reservation spot to someone further down on the list for a quick profit.

When I showed up Adam's place, he actually had one of the rare Ferraris parked in the garage, waiting to flip to its new owner, and we were checking it out while I talked to him about my plans to move down to Orange County.

I called Dad to tell him about the situation in San Francisco and my plans to move down to Newport Beach. I asked him where the condo was we lived when I was a kid and spent the summer with Misti back in the '80s. Dad couldn't remember the exact location but said it was somewhere close to South Coast Plaza. We talked about our memories from that summer while Dad lived in Costa Mesa for that brief period in time. I thought it was cool I was looking to move to the same area as a young man all these years later. I explained I was good financially for a little while but was actively looking for a new tech sales job in Orange County. Dad told me he would help out if needed and wished me all the best in my move.

I called Jennifer to tell her about all the changes happening in my life. It had been a little over a year at this point with us talking on a regular basis and exchanging frequent emails. I told her my reasoning in wanting to move to Orange County and how much I liked the area. Jennifer had moved out of her parents' house and into a place of her own. She was dating a guy, which was to be expected as she never had a shortage of guys after her. We always flirted and joked about how we were meant for each other but the distance between us made a committed relationship unrealistic.

I found a small townhouse in Costa Mesa that I liked with an older guy renting out the second bedroom. The bedroom for rent had its own bathroom and a small private deck. It was a month-to-month setup, and after I signed the paperwork, I rented a small moving truck to head up to San Francisco to pick up my furniture and bring it down to Costa Mesa.

Shortly after, I received a call for a potential opportunity to work for a small professional services company that focused on local software related projects. It was a sales position prospecting for one of the well know tech giants and aligning with their local sales team. I was excited to break into the ecosystem as they were a huge player in the tech industry. I was scheduled for my interview at their small office in Aliso Viejo. I really liked the office and got a great impression meeting with the leadership team. Everyone was dressed casually in the office except for those who were heading out to client meetings. The whole team seemed like they got along really well and had a lot of fun together. The president was a cool Asian guy who dressed really well and drove a dark green convertible Porsche. He had a surfboard hanging on the wall in his office so he could hit beach before or after work if the waves were good. I clicked with him right away, and he took me out to lunch for my interview. He saw something in me, telling me they would be thrilled to have me as part of their company. The company had made me an official offer within days, which I accepted and was excited to get started.

That first year with the company, I did well and really enjoyed the culture of the company, which almost felt like a family. I decided to move from Costa Mesa to Aliso Viejo as I found a similar setup right down the street from the office. The guy who owned the house in Aliso Viejo was an artist who, after a divorce, decided to rent out rooms in the house since he spent almost all of his time in the garage painting. The owner moved into the smallest room in the house and was renting out the six hundred square foot master suite. It was a much nicer room with a lower rent since Aliso Viejo was less expensive than Costa Mesa.

Shortly after the move, I received an email from Jennifer mentioning she would be in Palm Springs for a few days for work and would love to get together. Jennifer was now working for an interior design company that staged model homes. She mentioned that she would have a few days off while in town and was planning to visit one of her friends, Wendy, who lived in Long Beach. I suggested that the three of us meet for a fun night in Hollywood, and I would invite Jay to join us. We made plans to meet in Long Beach and then head up to Hollywood. I was looking forward to seeing Jennifer again as it had been almost two years since the last time we had seen each other in person.

# THE ONE

....................

I met Jennifer in Long Beach, and the attraction was immediate. As much as I tried to play it cool, I was crazy about her. The girls drove separately, following me to a bar that was a new hot spot on Hollywood Boulevard, and Jay arrived shortly after. We stayed at the same bar the whole night, drinking and having a great time together. As the night came to an end, Jay had found out about an after-party at a house up in the Hollywood Hills. It was getting late for Jennifer's friend Wendy, so she decided to head home while Jennifer, Jay, and I decided to go check out this party in the hills.

When we arrived at the house, we couldn't believe how nice the place was. It was a huge mansion, up in the hills, with an infinity pool, that overlooked Hollywood. It almost seemed unreal as to why anyone with a house like that would open it up to strangers. The house had bartenders ready to serve the party. As we walked around checking out the house, we just couldn't believe this was where the night had taken us.

I opened a door to the garage and found a gorgeous Bentley parked inside. As I checked out the car, I noticed a large roll of cash just sitting there on the center console. It felt like this whole thing must have been staged for a TV show or something. Who would leave cash like that just sitting out in the open and invite a bunch of random people over? We never did figure out who the house belonged to. As the early hours of the morning were approaching, Jay invited Jenn and me to stay at his place since one of his roommates was out of town and his room was open. At this point, Jenn and I didn't want to leave each other's side, so we all headed back to Jay's house to get some sleep before Jenn's flight back to Denver the next day. I drove Jenn to the airport in the morning to catch her flight. After spending the night together, it felt like things were now more than just a long-distance friendship.

I was back in the office with a serious case of the Monday blues. I couldn't stop thinking about my night with Jennifer and had no idea when I would be able to see her again. We continued to talk every day, and before the end of the week, I invited her to come stay with me for a weekend in Aliso Viejo. I wanted to show her where I lived, explaining it was much different than Hollywood. I mentioned my DJ gig at the Huntington Beach Brewery, my friend Travis set up for me, that was happening in a few weeks and how much I would love to have her there with me that Friday night. Jenn loved the idea and we started to coordinate her trip to spend a weekend with me. We sent each other emails during the day and talked every night leading up to our weekend together.

The day had finally come, I picked her up from the Orange County airport that Friday afternoon before my gig. We headed back to my place to have some drinks while I played some records, getting ready for my set later that night. I packed up my turntables & records and loaded them into the back of my truck with Jenn riding shotgun as we headed over to Huntington Beach Beer Company on Main Street. As the night went on, the place became more and more crowded with people. I loved having Jenn hanging out with me while I played a two-hour set of old-school hip-hop.

We spent the next day hanging around Laguna Beach. We sat on a patio of Nick's restaurant on the Pacific Coast Highway, having lunch and drinks enjoying the beautiful weather. I was so in love with Jennifer and had never had such strong feelings toward someone. Later that night, we ended up shooting pool and listening to a band play at the Marine Room, which is a classic beach bar right in the heart of Laguna Beach. I was sitting on a stool with Jenn sitting in between my legs on the edge of the stool while we waited for our next shot playing against another couple. I had this overwhelming sense of happiness that I was with the one. I had never felt so sure about something.

That Sunday, we had plans to hang out with Greg, one of my college buddies, who invited us to come hang out at his pool. Greg knew Jennifer from Colorado State and wanted to see her while she was in town. We spent the day sitting poolside with drinks, enjoying our remaining time together before Jenn's flight back to Denver. As it was getting close to take Jenn to the airport, I overheard her talking to someone on the phone in Greg's bedroom. It sounded serious, so I looked in to be sure everything was ok. Jenn gestured to me to give her a second.

After the call, I asked if everything was ok. She told me that we hadn't talked much about this, but she had been dating someone else back in Denver. She said that she called to break things off as she only wanted to be with me moving forward, even if it was a long-distance relationship. Even though I felt such strong chemistry between us, it was good to hear Jenn was feeling the same way. I drove Jenn to the airport to see her off back to Denver. I was sad that our weekend together had come to an end and was usure when I would see her next.

A few days later during one of our phone calls, I told her how much I had been thinking about our situation and wanted her to consider potentially moving in with me in Southern California. I told her that she didn't need to give me an answer right away, but I wanted to put it out there as to where my head was in our relationship. I mentioned how I needed to move out of the house that I was renting because the owner had decided to sell the house. I told her that I had been looking at apartments at this new complex right down the street from my office and found a place that I would be moving into shortly. I told her how much I would love to share the apartment together.

Jenn said it was a lot to consider, and as much as she wanted to be with me, she felt strongly that she shouldn't live with someone before being married. She said she needed to think about it further as she liked her apartment in Denver and her job. She said if she was to move to California, it would probably make more sense to consider finding a place with her friend Wendy in Long Beach. I really wanted us to live together and told her that I felt we were on a path to marriage. I wasn't expecting an answer right away, but it just felt good to tell her how I felt about us.

I called my parents to catch them up on the latest. I told Dad how crazy I was about Jennifer and told him I thought she was the one. I reminded him that he had met her at the bar during my college graduation party in Colorado and asked her how I could have ever broken up with someone as pretty as her. He could tell how crazy about her I was and was happy for me. When I called Mom to tell her, she immediately told me that she needed to meet this girl. She offered to fly us both down to Atlanta to spend a long weekend at the house. She told me that she would set up a barbeque at the house and invite all of their friends to meet Jennifer while we were in town. When I discussed this with Jenn, she loved the idea of seeing where I grew up and meeting my mom & Peter. I coordinated flights to fly to Denver, meet up with Jenn, and then we'd both fly to Atlanta. My mom picked up our tickets, and I couldn't wait to see Jennifer again.

We arrived in Atlanta to find Peter waiting for us. He was wearing a tight black T-shirt that barely covered his belly, with a pink silhouette of a girl like you see on truckers mud flaps that said "Badda Bing". I couldn't stop laughing at the T-shirt, joking with Peter on the drive back to the house about how much I appreciated him getting so dressed up to make a good first impression on Jennifer.

Mom & Peter had sold the Buckhead house, and had downsized into a house a few miles away in the Vinings area. The new house was a modern white stucco and glass structure that looked like an art museum or an office building. It was a really cool-looking house and the perfect place to showcase Peter's modern art collection. When we arrived at the house, Mom gave Jenn a big hug, telling her they had some catching up to do as she led her into the kitchen where there was a bottle of Patron tequila on the counter. Mom opened the bottle and poured a couple of shots for her and Jenn. Mom was so excited to get to know this girl that I was so crazy about. Mom and Jenn drank tequila, talking while I hung out with Peter, who cooked a nice dinner for all of us that evening.

The next day, I was eager to show Jenn around Atlanta. Mom let us have her car while in town, which was this sexy black-on-black two-door Jaguar convertible with a V8 engine. I immediately put the top down, showing Jenn around where I had grown up. I wanted her to see the house in Buckhead where I graduated high school before we met in college. Somebody else lived in the house, but I drove down the long driveway anyway for her to briefly see the house.

Seeing the Buckhead house brought back a lot of memories as I thought about where life had taken me since that day I headed off to college. I thought about if I hadn't chosen Colorado State, I would never have met Jennifer. We met Mom and Peter for lunch by the house at a restaurant called Canoe. Over lunch, Jenn and I couldn't keep our hands off each other, kissing every couple of minutes. Peter joked with me after lunch, saying I should tone the public affection down a bit as the whole restaurant was uncomfortable.

Later that afternoon, Jenn & I had tickets to Music Midtown, which was a large outdoor music festival in downtown. My friend Garrett, who drove with me out to college my first year, told me about the concert. He said a group of high school friends would be going and offered to drive us. We drove to Garrett's place and jumped in his car. We parked as close as possible. On our walk to the venue, an unexpected rainstorm came in out of nowhere. We were completely soaked within seconds. Without any shelter in sight, we started to run back to the car. We were laughing at how hard it was raining. It had happened so suddenly and we were soaked. We climbed into the car as the rain pounded down. Garrett had a little bag of blow with him. The three of us were soaking wet while we did a few lines on the center console. Hearing the sound of the heavy rain on the car was a beautiful sound. About twenty minutes later, the rain eased up enough for us to make it into a local bar to wait for the rain to stop so we could return to the music festival. Once the rain had completely stopped, we returned to the music festival, the bands started back up, and it was a great evening of music and me introducing Jenn to some of my old friends.

After a late night, we spent the next day relaxing and lounging around the Vinings house. We were in and out of the bedroom the whole day. That night, Mom and Peter took us out for a nice dinner and then drinks at Tongue & Groove. Our last day in Atlanta, Mom and Peter had coordinated a big barbeque at the house. I invited a group of my high school friends, and Mom and Peter invited their friends to meet Jennifer before we headed home the next morning. It was a hot and muggy day after all the rain, and we had a casual afternoon of good food and company. The next morning, we flew out. I dropped Jenn off in Denver and continued with my flight back to Orange County.

Back in my apartment, I was lonely without Jenn by my side. Now back to phone calls, we talked about how much we missed each other and how great it was to be together in Atlanta. Jenn mentioned she had a wedding coming up in a few weeks for one of her friends in Denver and wanted me to go with her. She thought it would be a great time for me to meet her parents while in town. I coordinated a roundtrip flight for that weekend and couldn't wait to see her again. When I landed in Denver, Jennifer picked me up from the airport, and we headed back to her place. She was living in a large house that had been converted into individual apartment units, and she lived on the top floor three stories up. That first night together, she cooked dinner for us and we went through a few bottles of wine.

The next day, we were to meet Jenn's parents for lunch, and I was kind of nervous as I really wanted them to like me. They were really nice, and as the lunch went on, I became more relaxed. It was obvious to them how much in love with each other we were. As we walked back to the car, Jenn told me that she could tell her parents really liked me. When we got back to the house, Jenn realized that she had locked her keys in her apartment. I asked if she had a window open, and she said, "The kitchen window has to be open, but it's on the third floor."

I stood back from the front of the house, plotting a way to get up to the window while getting back in touch with my ninja skills. I used the neighbor's fence to jump onto the roof of the first story, then managed to climb up to the second floor and then third floor, entering Jennifer's apartment through the kitchen window to unlock the door. Jennifer couldn't believe I was able to get into her apartment on the third floor through an outside window.

Jennifer was in the wedding, so she needed to be there early. I dropped her off at the wedding and planned to head over a few hours later. The wedding and reception were at an older house in Denver with the ceremony taking place in the backyard. During the reception while everyone was dancing, Jennifer grabbed my hand to come with her as she headed to the bathroom. I started to lean against the wall outside to wait for her, but she pulled me into the bathroom, and we had sex before the night started winding down.

The day after the wedding, we made plans to head up to Fort Collins for the day before catching my flight in the evening back to California. It was fun being with Jenn, driving around our old college town, talking about all our memories and favorite places from that period in our lives. We had lunch at the Pickle Barrel, which was a popular sandwich shop in town. We drove by our old dorms and the houses we lived in during our college years. We kept talking about how we would have never guessed that we would be back together all these years later after college.

Before heading back to Denver, we stopped by Sullivan's for a drink. We talked about being in the bar the night of my graduation party and Jennifer meeting Dad. It was crazy to be back in that bar and thinking about all of the changes in my life over the past five years. As my flight approached, we jumped back in Jennifer's car and headed toward the airport with the weekend coming to an end. Jennifer dropped me off at the Denver airport. We said our goodbyes in front of the terminal, without any plans when we would see each other next.

After about a week of emails and nightly calls, Jennifer told me that she had made up her mind. She wanted to move to California to be with me. She was still strong in her belief that she would need to find her own place or potentially live with her friend Wendy in Long Beach. I told her how much I loved her and I was convinced we were on a path toward marriage. I mentioned it would be easier for us both financially if we shared my one-bedroom apartment instead of paying separate rents. Jennifer really wanted to be sure I was thinking we were heading toward marriage if she was to move in with me, and I convinced her that was where my head was. Jennifer was almost ready to make the move but still needed to talk with her parents about her decision.

She went to her parents' house to tell them her thoughts and how she wanted to move to California to be with me. Jennifer's mom could tell by the way Jenn talked about us that it was the right decision; she'd had the exact opposite reaction when Jennifer talked with her about getting engaged and moving to San Diego with her fiancé after college. Jennifer's mom knew it was a mistake back then and cried for days, but this time around, she told Jennifer that it felt right. It was within weeks that Jennifer resigned from her interior design position in Denver, wrapped up her lease on her apartment, packed up her white Ford Explorer, and hit the road to Southern California to move in with me.

Jennifer arrived in Aliso Viejo, and I was so excited to have her with me full-time. I loved shopping with her picking out things to make our place feel like her own. She had such great taste. While unpacking her things, she showed me a scrap book that she had made printing out all of our email interactions over the past few years and she even still had the postcard with Brad Pitt I sent her during the summer of 96 while I was in Los Angeles. We were so in love with each other, and I felt such a peace falling asleep next to her at night.

It didn't take long for Jenn to find a new job as an assistant to a local interior designer who had a store in Corona Del Mar, which was the nicest part of Newport Beach. At this point, I didn't see any point in waiting to propose to Jenn, so I started to look into engagement rings. I reached out to my mom for guidance. I wasn't able to afford an expensive ring, so I asked Mom if she had any connections in Atlanta where I could get a diamond at a reasonable price. It was shortly after Mom called to tell me that someone on Peter's side of the family, who was a diamond collector, had a smaller nearly perfect emerald-cut diamond that he would sell to me at a very reasonable price. It sounded perfect, and I liked that the diamond was coming from someone within the family. I figured I could find a local jeweler in Orange County to decide on a setting for the diamond. The plan was in motion as I bought the diamond and had it shipped to my office.

I was always with Jennifer outside of work, but I wanted to tell her parents my thoughts and ask for their permission to propose. I really wanted to articulate my thoughts to them about how crazy I was about Jenn and our history together. I decided to write a well-worded email to them and then call them afterward. Jenn's parents were absolutely thrilled about the idea, and I felt at ease moving forward in planning out my proposal.

I kept thinking about that day when we reconnected over the phone while I was in San Francisco a few years after college. I was at sitting on the corner of Fillmore and Broadway overlooking the Bay when we reconnected, and I thought that would be a perfect place to propose. I liked the idea of taking a trip with Jennifer to San Francisco for a weekend, proposing in that same spot and then showing her my favorite places from when I lived there. The diamond arrived at the office, and I opened it at my desk right away. It wasn't a big diamond, but it was absolutely beautiful. I found local jeweler in Laguna Niguel and decided on a simple platinum setting. I brought up the idea of taking a trip up to San Francisco to Jenn, telling her how much I would love to show her around for a weekend. Jennifer had always wanted to live in San Francisco and was really excited to spend a weekend with me in the city. We determined a weekend that worked well, and I booked our airfare and a room at a boutique hotel in Union Square.

I had the ring in my coat pocket as I picked up Jennifer from work to catch our flight to San Francisco. I was hoping that the ring wouldn't cause any issues going through security at the Orange County Airport and ruin the surprise. We made it through without issue, but when we landed in San Francisco, Jennifer asked for my coat as she was cold. I was caught off-guard and was a completely unexpected twist. I thought it would have been obvious if I took something out of my coat pocket before handing my coat to Jenn, so I abruptly said I needed to hit the bathroom real quick. While in the bathroom, I took the ring from my coat and put it in my pants pocket. As I walked out, I handed my coat to Jenn.

As we arrived in the city, it was a dreary night that was foggy and misty. Jenn was feeling a little under the weather, so she suggested we just stay in for the night. I had big plans that night, so I convinced her to at least head out for a drink together. As we closed out our tab at a local bar, I told her there was one more place I wanted to show her right down the street before we headed back to the hotel. We walked a few blocks to the corner of Fillmore and Broadway. As we stood there, I explained the background behind that street corner and how it was the location where I spoke to her for the first time when we reconnected after college. I told her how I had never felt the way I did about her with anyone else, how happy I was when we were together, and how much I loved her. I pulled the ring from my pocket and proposed. Jennifer was surprised and overwhelmed with excitement as she hugged me with an enthusiastic "Yes." The dreary conditions added to the unique beauty of that night. I told Jenn that I had reserved a booth at an upscale bar down the hill a few blocks for us to celebrate. We held hands as we walked down the long staircase on the side of Fillmore to the bar. When we walked in, told the host my name for the reservation and they escorted us to a little private room that had a silver bucket with champagne on ice. After we finished the bottle, we walked around to a few more bars on Union Street to continue our celebration before heading back to our hotel for the night.

Back in Aliso Viejo, we started planning for our wedding. We decided on a winter wedding in Vail, Colorado, at the end of February. We liked Colorado since it would be central for people to travel from the East Coast and West Coast. I loved the idea of being able to spend a few days skiing out on the mountain with family and friends before the ceremony. Jenn and I were anxious to make it official as soon as possible, so we decided it would be the upcoming winter, about six months out. Given that the wedding would be peak ski season, we had to accept the fact that everything was going to be expensive. We decided our best option was to reserve a single location for both the ceremony and reception. We decided on the Larkspur restaurant right at the base of the mountain in the Lions Head village. We had only seen pictures online but liked the fireplace in the restaurant and wanted that to be the backdrop as we exchanged our vows. Everything was in motion, and our focus was on planning for our wedding.

A few months prior to our wedding, the executive team at my company thought I was ready for the next step in my career. They asked if I had any interest in going to work for the tech giant that we supported as they were looking to add to their sales team in San Francisco and they could help me secure a position. They said going to work for a company of their size would provide much more opportunity for advancement, and they liked the idea having me on the inside with potential to steer business their way. I was excited about the potential opportunity but needed to discuss with Jennifer as this would be quite a change for her, considering she had just moved from Denver and found a new position in Orange County. That night, I brought up the idea, and she was really excited about it. She told me that she had always wanted to live in San Francisco. She told me that she had considered moving to San Francisco a couple of years after college, because she heard I had moved there, and hoped to run into me in the city.

The next day when I went into the office, I told my executive team that I wanted to pursue the opportunity with the tech giant further. Through their connections, I was scheduled right away for an interview at their corporate office just outside of San Francisco. Through the positive referral of my company along with the tech giant's sales team I had been aligned with in Southern California, I was offered the position after a handful of interviews. It was time to put things in motion for the move up to San Francisco and find a new place.

# CITY LIFE 2.0

. . . . . . . . . . . . . . . . . .

We were set on living in downtown and took a trip up to San Francisco to look at apartments. Considering a big portion of my monthly income would be commission, which would take some time to ramp up, and it would take Jennifer some time to find a job in the city, we were looking for places with reasonable rent. Even the lowest rent apartments in the city were considerably more than Aliso Viejo in Orange County. We found an apartment building we liked that was newly renovated for reasonable rent, but it was close to Sixth Street, which was the worst street in the city. We were originally interested in their loft apartments, which were open floor plans with an upstairs loft area, but there weren't any available. We decided on a traditional apartment in the building and signed a year lease.

After we returned to Aliso Viejo to start packing for the move, we received a call from the leasing office in San Francisco as they had one of their loft apartments open up. We jumped all over it as they didn't stay available long, and the front office changed our lease over to the loft. As we packed up everything in Aliso Viejo, we decided that we would only need one car living in the city, so I sold Jennifer's white Ford Explorer. We rented a moving truck, loaded up what little furniture we had at the time, and hit the road up to San Francisco.

We arrived in the city after dark. We checked in with the front office, who handed over our keys, and were told all the lofts were ground floor in the back alley. We hadn't gotten a chance to see one of the lofts in person while we were there before as none were available. When we pulled up to the loft, we felt uneasy as our front door was right on a sketchy alley half a block from the worst street in all of San Francisco. We opened up the back of the moving truck to start moving our stuff in, and a guy on the streets offered to help and wouldn't go away. It probably wasn't the smartest move allowing a stranger to help and seeing everything go into the apartment, but I was exhausted and wanted to get moved in as quickly as possible. I gave him some cash for his help, and once everything was in, we closed ourselves into our new place.

Our space was far from what we envisioned living in a cool downtown loft would be like. That first month was a culture shock, especially with what the alley outside our door was like at night. At night, cars were broken into right outside our door, setting off alarms on a regular basis. From time to time, the red-and-blue lights from police cars lit up our loft through the windows. All through the night, you could hear constant foot traffic right outside the door.

One evening while we were watching TV, the doorbell kept ringing. I opened the door and came face to face with a guy holding his boom box, unaware he was pressed right up against the doorbell on the wall. I kindly asked if he could maybe find another spot to lean against the wall, and the guy stumbled off down the alley. We never opened the blinds for fear it would provide clear visibility of all of our stuff. Even when it was a nice day outside, we kept the windows shut as the alley smelled of urine.

I had no choice but I was extremely uncomfortable leaving Jenn alone in our loft when I had to travel for work from time to time for a few days. I would talk to Jenn over the phone at night while away to comfort her until she fell asleep. I felt responsible for the situation putting us in that loft and worried it would have a negative impact on our relationship. I felt bad that I had asked Jennifer to move from a place she liked in Denver and now, only a few months after her move, we were living in such a rough area. The shining light was our upcoming wedding, which was now only a few weeks away. We were both looking forward to spending time with family and friends in the mountains of Vail, Colorado.

# WINTER WEDDING

....................

We arrived in Vail three days before the wedding and checked into the Lodge at Vail. Our room had a balcony on the second floor that overlooked the main street that ran through Vail Village. When I stepped out onto the balcony, I saw a crew setting up a stage thirty feet from our balcony for what looked to be an après-ski event that would take place that evening. We reached out to our wedding party, inviting anyone in town to come to our room for drinks and a perfect spot to check out the band on the balcony. It was a perfect way to kick off the celebration for the next few days. My parents didn't arrive until the next day, and I couldn't wait to see them.

Leading up to the ceremony, I spent the next few days out on the mountain with everyone who was skiing while in town. Jenn spent those days relaxing in the local spas, preparing for the big day. The day before our wedding, I was able to break away with Dad, and just the two of us spent the whole afternoon skiing together. I loved being out on the mountain with Dad, following each other down the mountain crisscrossing back and forth across the runs. We finished the day with some beers in the lodge for après-ski.

Dad told me how proud of me he was and couldn't believe the time had come where I was about to get married. He told me, how much he liked Jennifer and thought we made a great couple. He loved skiing Vail, and thought the back bowls were one of the prettiest places he had ever skied. I thought about my first trip to Vail; I was just starting my life in college when I got my season pass. I would have never guessed that ten years later, I would be in Vail, about to marry Jennifer, whom I met for the first time during my sophomore year and skiing with Dad before the wedding. That evening, we had reserved a private area in the Tap Room, which was a nice bar and restaurant in Vail

Village, for the wedding party to all get together. It was a mellow evening of us just enjoying time with the wedding party before the big day.

The morning of our wedding, Jenn and I had breakfast together at the Sonnenalp Hotel before she headed to the salon to get her hair and makeup done. We met back at our room to get ready together before heading over to the Larkspur for the ceremony and reception. Jennifer looked absolutely stunning in her sexy, thin white silk dress. She had hair extensions put in at the salon, which made her hair look thick like a lion's mane. It was snowing hard the day of the wedding, so the little ski town was covered in a blanket of snow. We took the hotel shuttle together over to the Larkspur for our ceremony and reception. Watching Jennifer walk through the snow holding up her white dress to keep it from dragging in the snow was such a beautiful sight.

We arrived early before our guests. The dining area and chairs were set up theater style facing the fireplace. The staff had set up a private reserved area for Jennifer to wait out of sight until it was time to walk down the aisle. We had about 70 people in town for the wedding, everyone started filtering into The Larkspur and looked great dressed up for the special day. People grabbed a glass of champagne in the bar area and mingled with each other briefly, awaiting the ceremony that was to start shortly. As the time had come, I joined Paster Tommy at the front of the room by the fireplace while everyone filtered in to take their seats. As the Beatles song "In My Life" started to play, Jennifer walked down the aisle and looked absolutely gorgeous. She joined me in front of the fireplace as we held hands, standing face to face. I couldn't believe I was about to be married to this beautiful girl standing in front of me. After a few words from Paster Tom, we exchanged our vows, ending with a big kiss while everyone cheered loudly. We made our way back down the center aisle together and into the bar area, ready to celebrate. A few minutes later, everyone followed behind and filtered into the reception area. While everyone mingled, The Larkspur staff worked to convert the dining room back into round tables and chairs for everyone in preparation for dinner. During dinner, Jenn and I loved looking around and seeing our family & friends mixed together and everyone enjoying the night.

After dinner, Peter stood up for a toast. He was a great public speaker and always captivated an audience. He told a story that he loved and told often from when I was sixteen. We ran into each other in the driveway as I was heading out for the night to meet up with friends. He liked the way I was dressed, told me how cool I looked, and asked if I had protection with me, referring to a condom. I had responded immediately with "Of course, I always keep a knife under my seat."

In his speech, he talked about watching me grow into a young man over the years and how perfect he thought Jennifer and I were for each other. Everyone loved his speech, and as the dinner came to an end, everyone made their way back into the bar area for the cutting of the cake and to celebrate over drinks. Dad wanted to handle the bar tab for the night but was cautious about the bill getting too out of hand. He gave the bartender approval to initially keep it as an open bar up until $5,000 and then check with him on keeping the tab open. Everyone was enjoying themselves, drinking, celebrating, sharing stories from the past and taking pictures. The bar tab reached the $5,000 mark, so the bartender looked over at Dad while he and I were talking at the end of the bar together. Dad gave the bartender a thumbs-up to keep the tab open for another $1,000 with a content look on his face. He loved buying drinks for people and seeing everyone have a good time.

The drinks were flowing, and as the tab approached the new limit, the bartender would look over at Dad, who gave the thumbs-up for another $1,000. As the evening was coming to an end, the tab ended up at a little over $7,000. As the bartender went to close down the tab, Dad's card bounced as it was such a large unexpected out-of-state transaction. It was too late, and Dad didn't want to deal with calling his card to see if he could get it sorted out. He was kind of embarrassed but asked Aunt Denise's husband, Rick, and a few others if they could help to cover the tab in which he would pay them back once situated back in Detroit.

As we closed down the restaurant, a group of us decided to catch last call at a bar in Vail Village. Jenn was walking through the snow-covered ski town still in her wedding dress and a long white suede coat with fur on the collar.

After last call, Jenn and I made our way back to our hotel room. We sat on the bed, looking through all of the wedding cards and everyone's generous gifts. We ended our night having sex as newlyweds before catching an early morning flight back to San Francisco so we could repack our bags before our honeymoon in Kauai, Hawaii.

We arrived back in San Francisco and took the underground subway from the airport to a stop on Market Street, which was close walking distance to our loft. As we came up the escalator to street level with our luggage, the reality set in of how much different of an environment it was where we lived versus the snowy ski village of Vail we had just left.

As we walked back to our loft, we stopped by an ATM to deposit all of our wedding cash. It was a little uncomfortable depositing so much cash on the street in such a rough area. We looked around to make sure no one was around, then quickly loaded all the cash into the machine, feeling relieved once it was all deposited. I told Jennifer that with the wedding money and having a better handle on my new job, I would look for a new place as soon as we returned from our honeymoon. Jennifer said now that the wedding was behind us, she could focus on finding a job in the city. She wanted to work for one of the luxury retail stores in Union Square. We arrived back at the loft, unpacked our dress clothes, and repacked our bags with all casual beach attire. We had a relaxing night talking about the wedding, got a good night's sleep, and headed back to the airport in the morning to catch our flight to Kauai.

We arrived in Hawaii to dreary rainy weather as it was late winter. When we got to our room, we found Mom & Peter had a bottle of champagne on ice waiting for us. The weather didn't bother us as it gave us an excuse to spend most of our time in bed. We spent the week enjoying the nicest restaurants the island had to offer and beach barhopping, going from shelter to shelter in between the rain showers. We rented a Jeep one day and drove up and down the coast. It was a relaxing week of us just enjoying being newlyweds.

# LOVE & LUXURY

....................

When we returned to San Francisco, I was focused on finding us a better living situation. I put an ad out to sublease our loft while I looked around for lofts in a better part of town. Each morning as I headed to the office, Jenn walked around Union Square, applying for jobs at the luxury retail stores. With her looks and personality, it didn't take long, and she was offered a full-time job at Louis Vuitton in Union Square. I found a new building that had just been finished with loft apartments a few blocks from the new San Francisco Giants baseball stadium. It was an up-and-coming area because of the ballpark. They also opened a Whole Foods nearby, which made it feel even more like a neighborhood. Through my ad on Craigslist, I found someone who was interested in subleasing our current loft as an office space.

I took Jenn to tour the new loft building, and we looked at all of the available units. We fell in love with this second-story loft that faced the front entrance on Brannan Street. It had twenty-foot ceilings, floor to ceiling windows, concrete pillars, wood floors, exposed pipes, and stainless steel appliances. It was a gorgeous space, and even though it was only seven hundred square feet, it felt large with the high ceilings. When you walked in the door, you walked down a steel staircase down onto the main floor. We would be the first tenants to occupy the unit. The loft was the most expensive option of the places we looked at, but with Jenn's new job and me seeing a better sales pipeline for potential commission, we felt comfortable that we could afford it, so we signed a year lease. The new loft was only five blocks from the old one, but the neighborhood felt like a night and day difference. The new loft would only be a twenty- to twenty-five-minute walk for Jennifer to Louis Vuitton. We couldn't get into the new loft fast enough and moved our stuff down the street into our new space. It was such a relief to be in a nicer area and have a place more in line with how we envisioned our life together in the city.

A few months later, Dad flew out to San Francisco as he wanted to spend a weekend with us to see our new place in the city. He arrived Friday evening, and we took him out for dinner and drinks at the Redwood Room in the Clift Hotel, which was a swanky restaurant and lounge in Union Square. I could tell Dad was impressed where we had settled in the city and loved to see how happy we were together. After dinner, Jennifer got up to head to the bathroom, and as we watched her walk away, Dad turned to me, telling me how well I had done as he thought she was such a beautiful girl while he picked up the check.

The next day, the plan was to take Dad on a bike ride through the city, over the Golden Gate Bridge to Sausalito, and then take the ferry back. During my previous period of living in San Francisco when I was single, I used to tell Dad all the time how much I loved riding over the bridge, and he would tell me it was something he always wanted to do. I was excited to make one of Dad's bucket list experiences happen. I rented him a comfortable bike, and we met at our loft while Jennifer was at work that day. I took him on my usual ride through the city, being a tour guide and pointing out all my favorite places. I showed him the spot where I had proposed to Jennifer. We rode through the Marina District, and I wanted to stop into my favorite bar, which was called Bar None. It was a casual bar that was down below street level. It felt like a college bar as it attracted a younger crowd. We locked up our bikes to a light post on the street and headed down into the bar for a few drinks.

It was a beautiful day outside, and the sun brightened up the front half of the bar with the front doors and windows open. Just like in Detroit with Dad on the vending route, I played some music on the jukebox while we talked about old times and everything leading up to my life in San Francisco. After our pit stop, we headed back up to the street with a slight buzz, unlocked our bikes, and continued with the ride. We rode along the bay, heading toward the Golden Gate Bridge, which was always a sight to see close up. We rode to the middle of the bridge, and I wanted to get a picture of Dad to document the experience of making one of his dreams a reality. I asked Dad to hold our bikes while I stepped back to get a few photos. We hung out in the middle of the bridge, taking a break while I told him how I used to ride out to this place all the time in the past, just taking in the view and appreciating my life in the city.

We continued across the bridge and down through the little town of Sausalito on the water. We sat on a patio and had a few more drinks while we waited for our ferry back to the city. When the ferry docked in the city, it was only a short ride back to our loft. With only a few hours before dinner, Dad took a taxi back to his hotel to get ready for dinner. That evening, we took him to Foreign Cinema, one of our favorite restaurants. It was a dark, fancy restaurant that projected foreign movies on the exterior wall of the white brick building next door. Each of the tables had little speakers for the sound of the movie being projected on the building. It was a great way to end Dad's trip to San Francisco before he caught his flight home to Detroit the next day.

In those early years of our marriage, we loved experiencing everything San Francisco had to offer and enjoying the finer things in life. Jennifer was recruited from Louis Vuitton to work across the street at Gucci, working with high-end clients and celebrities who were in town. I continued to excel in my sales career, being awarded as a top performer multiple years, which provided an income level for us to live comfortably.

Considering our dual income, one car, and no kids, we took trips wherever we wanted and lived the good life. I traded in the Montero for a new dark blue Audi A4. It felt good to be able to stroll into the dealership and buy such a nice car. I started to appreciate nice watches and bought a beautiful Tag Heuer Link Chronograph. During the week, we usually spent our evenings dining out around San Francisco, catching up on our day at work. We took trips to the wine country and stayed at relaxing spas during the summer. I sold my mountain bike and bought a road bike to ride around the city. I joined a local boxing gym, between biking and learning to box I was in great shape. I wanted to get back into Snowboarding, bought a new Burton board and we started taking trips to Lake Tahoe in the winter. Jennifer didn't ski or snowboard but still really liked staying at the resorts, relaxing at the spas, and shopping while I headed out onto the mountain for the day.

Considering Jennifer's time working at Louis Vuitton and then Gucci, she utilized her employee discount and always dressed to the nines. She looked at her wardrobe as an investment, buying classic pieces that were timeless. She bought things she could wear for the rest of her life and even potentially hand down to our daughter someday.

We wanted to get a puppy together, and since we didn't have the space for a large dog in our little loft, Jenn convinced me to get a little dog. We found this Chihuahua-Pomeranian puppy online and fell in love with his photos. We had him shipped to us and named him Brannan after the street we lived on. We loved him so much, taking him for walks around the city and to the local parks. It was such a great time in our lives, enjoying our early years of marriage in the city.

We liked taking weekend trips down to Hollywood to meet up with my friend Adam and his wife Michelle, during the summer months. We enjoyed staying at The Standard, The Roosevelt, and The Mondrian Hotel's, soaking up the sun poolside during the day and then hitting the trendy hot spots at night. I loved the Sunset Strip, and it was fun to experience it this time around when I was doing well and could afford lavish nights out, compared to my first year after college.

We had a memorable weekend staying at The Standard Hotel on the Sunset Strip. It was a gorgeous summer day in LA as we started our weekend poolside with drinks listening to the DJ. Before we knew it, we had made friends with another group of couples sitting by the pool who invited us up to their room as they had some cocaine with them. Throughout the day, we would head up to the room for a bit and then back down to the pool for the next round of drinks. While hanging around the pool, I recognized a guy from a Mountain Dew commercial that I liked. I went over and asked if that was him in the commercial; he introduced himself to me as Channing Tatum. He was an unknown actor at the time, and I told him I thought he was cool in the commercial. There was something about him, I felt like he was going to be big someday. We made small talk for a bit, talking about how fun the pool party was, and Channing asked for my number to potentially meet up while out on the town later that night. I never heard from him, and my friend Jay loved to tease me how I gave my number out to a guy who became *People's* Sexiest Man Alive, but he never called.

That evening, we headed out with our new friends from the pool party for a night on the town. They had rented a stretched Hummer limousine for the night and invited us to join them. The Hummer was so long Adam and I joked about how it didn't even need to drive anywhere. We could just enter in the back, walk to the front, and get out at the next club. We spent the night barhopping with our new friends all along the strip into the early morning hours.

The next morning, we all met for a late breakfast back poolside, completely hungover. Over breakfast, Michelle asked Jenn if she wanted to take a drive in Adam and Michelle's new Porsche down to Rodeo Drive. Adam and I looked at each other with the same thing going through our minds. Adam encouraged the girls to take the car, handing over the keys. As we wrapped up breakfast, Michelle and Jenn headed out. As we watched the girls head out, I asked Adam if we still had any blow from last night. He told me he was thinking the same thing. I said, "Let's close this tab down and head up to the room." Adam picked up the check and signed the bill as "Big time fucking movie producer, Lee Donowitz" who was a character in the movie *True Romance*.

It was a gorgeous morning with the sun shining in through the balcony, the DJ had just started back up, and we were ready to get the party started again to cancel out our hangovers. As we chopped up some lines, I put on Soundgarden's "Outshined" on my Bluetooth speaker, wanting to recreate the same vibe as Brad Pitt smoking weed from the honey bear bong in the movie *True Romance*. We were looking forward to one more day by the pool before ending the weekend.

It was shortly after, we heard a room card inserted into the lock to open the door. We panicked, Adam placing one of the hotel magazines over the lines of blow, and the girls entered the room. We were caught completely off-guard, thinking the girls would be gone for hours strolling Rodeo Drive, but it was just a quick trip for Michelle to return something. The girls immediately knew something was up with the music blasting while we seemed suspicious. Jenn laughed as she asked, "What was going in here?" It was obvious what we were up to, and after a good laugh, we all proceeded to start up another party day by the hotel pool before heading home in the morning.

One afternoon in San Francisco while picking Jennifer up from Gucci, I was browsing through the store, waiting for her to get off of work. I came across this men's Gucci watch with a brown crocodile band, black face, and silver *G*-shaped bezel. I immediately thought about Dad as it looked similar to a watch he used to wear when I was a little kid. Dad had bought his and hers matching Cartier Tank watches that had gold bezels and brown crocodile bands for himself and Mom when they were married. The Gucci watch reminded me of those watches. I thought about how cool it would be to buy Dad something nice now that I was doing well, considering how much he had done for me over the years. Jenn saw me checking out the watch in the glass case and asked if I liked it. I told her I wanted to buy it for Dad and asked if it was something she could get with her discount. Jenn looked into it and was able to get a pretty substantial discount on it. Before I committed to buying the watch, I wanted to be sure Dad liked it and would actually wear it before spending the money. I asked Jenn if she could put it on hold while I showed a picture from the website to Dad later that evening.

I called Dad when I got home to talk to him about the watch. I caught him while he was in the van servicing his customers. I told him about the watch and how I wanted to get it for him but wanted to show it to him first. Of course, he appreciated the gesture but told me I didn't need to buy him anything. I didn't accept his response, insisting that I really wanted to get it for him. I told him I wanted him to see a picture on Gucci's website to be sure he liked it and would wear it before I bought it. He told me that he would be home in a few hours and would check it out. He said he wasn't good with computers, but Jack was, so he asked me to call Jack at the house to set it all up. I called Jack at the house right away, told him the situation, and emailed him a link to photos of the watch on the Gucci website. When Dad arrived back at the house, I called him and told him Jack had everything set up in the office on the computer. While on the phone, Dad went upstairs into the office to see the pictures. I could hear the excitement in his voice as he said, "Well hell, yeah, I like that watch!" I knew he would but just wanted confirmation. Dad said he wouldn't wear it to work but would wear it out on special occasions. It was a done deal, so the next day, I asked Jenn to get the watch and had it shipped to Dad's house. Sending Dad the watch made me feel so good being at a point in my life where I could buy him something nice to show my appreciation for everything he had done for me over the years.

After our first three years of marriage in downtown San Francisco, we started talking about settling down and starting a family. We couldn't imagine raising a child in the city being so expensive and space was limited. Even living outside of the city, houses were extremely expensive in the Bay Area. We were focused on the potential to move back down to Orange County, which we thought would be a better place to raise a family. I was ready to take the next step in my career and talked with my sales leadership about a potential new sales role back down in Southern California. They were always looking for sales reps, so I pursued openings that would allow me to be based back down in Orange County. There were a few openings, and I was offered a new role covering San Diego, which would allow me to live anywhere in Southern California. Orange County was a perfect location to settle down as it was in the middle of Los Angeles and San Diego, which kept the door open for future opportunities. I accepted the offer, Jenn and I made our plans to make our way back down south to Orange County.

# BEACH TOWN ROOTS

We put our focus on moving to the Costa Mesa/Newport Beach area to plant our roots. I knew we would need to get another car as part of the move and wanted to surprise Jenn with something cool for her. I loved Audi's and thought Jennifer would look hot driving a little Audi TT convertible with the top down wearing her big sunglasses. After shopping around, I found a few year-old silver with black leather interior convertible TT in like new condition and low miles for a reasonable price in Los Angeles. It made me think of the silver Corvette Dad had bought Mom before I was born. I told Jenn that I had to take a quick trip down to Southern California for a training as part of my transition into the new role. I flew down to Los Angeles, took a taxi to the dealer, paid cash for the Audi, drove it down to Orange County, and parked it in Adam's garage until our move back down the coast. When I returned to San Francisco, I couldn't keep my excitement about the car a secret, so over dinner one night, I told Jennifer why I really flew down to Los Angeles and showed her pictures of the car. She was so excited about the car and having a little convertible to cruise around in sunny Southern California.

We packed up our San Francisco loft and loaded up the moving truck, which my company took care of as part of my relocation. We decided to stay an extra night at a hotel in San Francisco while our stuff was being driven down to Southern California so we could have one last night out on the town with friends. Jenn's colleagues from Gucci wanted to take her out for her last night to wish her well on the next chapter in her life. I wanted to spend some time with some of my friends in the city, so we split up for the evening and planned to meet back at the hotel.

Early the next morning, I was awoken to Jennifer nudging me, and she looked really worried about something. It was a shock to wake up from a deep sleep and see her like that as it seemed like she was really concerned. When I asked what was wrong, she said that she had suspected she might be pregnant, so she took a pregnancy test but hadn't looked at the result yet. She said she was so nervous, and the test was sitting on the bathroom counter. The news woke me up pretty quick as I headed toward the bathroom. While wiping my eyes of sleep, I was still in shock about what was going on. I picked up the test; it read positive. I walked into the room with the test in my hand and said, "We're having a baby!" Worry turned into delight as we thought about the fact that we were going to be parents. After hugging and kissing, I headed back into the bathroom to shower for the day. In the shower, I was filled with so much excitement that I was going to be a father as I thought about how much I loved Jennifer and being in the process of moving back down to Southern California.

We took our time on our drive down to Orange County as it was expected that it would take up to a week for the moving truck to arrive with our furniture. We stayed a few nights in a luxury hotel on the beach in Santa Barbra. When we arrived, we spent a few nights at Adam and Michelle's house in Newport Beach. I showed Jenn her new Audi TT parked in the garage, and she absolutely loved it. Our plan was to rent an apartment over the next year while we got situated back in Orange County and spend some time looking at houses before deciding where we wanted to plant our roots. We rented a one-bedroom apartment at the Newport Bluffs apartment complex, which were luxury apartments that had a beautiful resort-style pool area. That year, the focus was on Jenn's pregnancy with multiple trips to the hospital to check on the baby.

A few months into her pregnancy, the time had come where we could find out the sex of the baby. We headed to the hospital for the ultrasound, and while standing around the monitor, the doctor revealed that we would be having a baby boy! I was so excited that I was going to have a son and a little buddy to take snowboarding, mountain biking, and surfing while we lived by the beach. After discussing a few different options for names, we both really liked the name Jake. I liked the name because the owner of Burton Snowboards was Jake Burton. We decided Jake would carry my same middle name, so his full name would be Jake Douglas Langley. Over the next six months, we spent most of our free time shopping for baby clothes and getting everything ready for Jake to join us. Toward the end of Jenn's pregnancy, she had a few professional photos taken by a local photographer, which were absolutely stunning. Through the photographer's connections, one of the photos was published in a local Newport Beach magazine and even ended up as a framed photo in the lobby of one of the local doctor's offices. As things were getting close to Jennifer's due date, it became obvious that her two door convertible wasn't going to work, and she needed a mom car, so I traded in the Audi TT for a white Lexus RX 330 SUV.

It was about ten days past Jennifer's due date when one night, the pain was unbearable, and we knew it was time. I drove us to the hospital in the early morning, and we checked into our room at Hoag Hospital. The rooms at Hoag were like a luxury hotel room with views of the Newport Beach coastline. I wasn't sure how I would be able to handle the sight of Jennifer giving birth, but as things progressed, I was so caught up in the moment that I wanted nothing more than to watch my son being born into the world. At the first sight of Jake's head, the doctor commented how blond his hair was. After Jake came into our world, we took turns holding our baby boy, overwhelmed with excitement and completely in love with him.

After a few days at the hospital with friends and family stopping by to meet Jake, it was time to take Jake home. The car ride home felt so different having a delicate baby in the car, so I took side streets and drove extra slow. When we got settled back at the apartment, I told Jenn I wanted to go get a tattoo of Jake's name on me. Jennifer wasn't crazy about tattoos but knew it was something that I wanted, and we had talked about it for months leading up to Jake's birth. Jennifer said she was fine with Jake, so I headed out to a local tattoo parlor in Newport Beach right next to Hoag Hospital. I told the shop I wanted Jake's name and birthdate over my heart on my left breast. The artist drew it up, I approved, laid down in the chair, and had Jake's name tattooed on me.

Those first six months, we adjusted to raising a baby boy. It made the apartment very peaceful as we were always trying to keep things, quiet playing kids' shows and music. We tried our best to get as much sleep as possible during the night, but Jenn pretty much took all the responsibility as I needed sleep to head out to work during the day. As the one-year lease came due for renewal on our apartment, we really wanted to find a house to give us more space and a separate bedroom for Jake.

Since the move down to Orange County, I had started surfing with Adam off the coast of Newport Beach when I could break away. Adam bought me a surfboard as a gift because he thought I would love it with my background in skateboarding. He expected me to excel at surfing right away, but it was a much different sport than skateboarding, and it took me longer than expected to pick it up. One day while sitting out in the ocean on our boards and waiting for the waves to roll in, we were talking about the local real estate market. Adam had multiple projects going on with his custom home building business and mentioned he was in the final stages of a small twelve-house development in East Costa Mesa called Canoe Pond. Real estate was expensive in Orange County, and I asked Adam's opinion, if he felt it was a good time for me to buy my first house. It was a big decision, and the monthly mortgage would be considerably more than rent on our one-bedroom apartment. Adam told me it was a strange time in the market, but real estate always does well in the long run, so if I planned to stay in the house for at least ten years, I'd do fine even if things went down in the short-term. Adam said he could help get the best price possible on one of the Canoe Pond houses and help with upgrades in the final build-out.

After looking at the available houses in Canoe Pond, we were most attracted to this little gray-and-white house in the front of the neighborhood;

the interior was unfinished, allowing us to pick out our own finishings to make it our own. It was a two-story 1700 square foot three-bedroom house on a 1900 square foot lot with a very small back patio. We picked out all of our finishings and were giving a final price to move forward. The market was in the beginning stages of a downturn, so we negotiated the price down a bit and got it to a point where the developer wouldn't budge any lower. I applied and was qualified for a loan on the house. Everything lined up pretty close for the Canoe Pond house to be ready right around the same time our lease was up on the apartment. We were so excited to have a little house to call our own to raise Jake.

In the months leading up to move-in, we loved shopping for furniture for Jake's room and the basics to accommodate a larger space. It was a regular thing for Jenn and I to take Jake at night to go look at what had been done to the house over the past few days. It was fun to watch the build-out and see it all come together as we imagined living together in our own house as a family. We closed on the house in November of 2007, just before the holidays and were able to spend our first Thanksgiving, Christmas, and New Year's as a family in our new house on Canoe Pond.

# OCEAN REFLECTIONS

·····················

It was at the end of the summer in 2009 and I was sitting on my surfboard off the coast of San Onofre on a beautiful sunny day waiting for the waves to roll in. I was just close enough to the shoreline where I could see Jennifer sitting in a beach chair under an umbrella while watching Jake play with sand toys on the beach. It was close to Dad's trial, that we had been waiting for about a year and a half, to hear the details as to what happened at his house on February 27th, 2008 with hopes that it may bring closure and some kind of justice. I was doing my best to just move on as there was nothing that could be done to bring Dad back. As I sat in the ocean with my legs in the water off the sides of my board I reflected on our life since moving into our house on Canoe Pond and hearing for the first time what had happened at Dad's Riverview house.

The past year and a half were a mix of working through what had been the toughest period of my life balanced out by the beautiful life I had with Jennifer & Jake. It seemed like right at the same time of losing Dad the country began what was an extremely rough period with the great recession. I felt my life had been pretty easy leading up to that point. I had bought our first house for my family at the end of 2007, which was in the early phase of one of the worst real estate market downturns in decades. As the value declined on our new house, I had to quit paying attention to the local home values. I kept telling myself we needed a place to live and brighter days were ahead. I had struggled in my own business as most of the companies in my sales territory were putting projects on hold or had made the decision to not invest in new large software systems. I tried to focus on the important things in life, which was my family. I loved being a father, and was married to the love of my life. Jennifer was so supportive during this period, always keeping a positive attitude.

I was constantly thinking about how the age difference between me and Jake was the exact same as me and Dad. When doing things with Jake, I saw myself as my dad and Jake as me when I was a kid. I had a strange moment in the car one day when I went to look into my rearview mirror, and seeing my forehead in the mirror, I thought I was looking at Dad's forehead. It caught me off-guard as I was overwhelmed with the feeling that I was now my dad or he was now part of me.

There were many weekend afternoons where I would play the best of Elton John or Rod Stewart in the house as their music reminded me of Dad and made the house feel like he was there. Elton John's "Rocket Man" was still coming on the radio at the most random places and times, which always made me feel like Dad was with me.

In the spring of 2009, I traded my blue Audi for a Jeep Wrangler. I wanted a lower maintenance vehicle to avoid costly repairs during the recession. I liked the idea of getting back to my roots and wanted one of the new four-door Jeep Wranglers. I still loved Jeeps ever since my dark blue Jeep in high school, and they had only continued to get better and more comfortable over the years. The new four-door model that came out in '07 made a Jeep a much better fit for the family. I wanted a cool surf truck for trips to the beach, camping, or skiing in the mountains. I couldn't wait to start skiing with Jake and be able to take trips with him like I had with Dad over the years. After hunting for the perfect Jeep, I found a dark green 2007 Wrangler Unlimited with a hardtop at my local dealer. I found so much joy that day, walking into the dealership and driving off with a modern version of my high school Jeep. As part of the final sale, I had the Jeep lifted with 35" BFG tires and it looked tough. Jake loved the Jeep and associated it with doing fun things with Dad. It made me think about how Dad had always been a Cadillac guy and I had always been attracted to Jeep Wranglers. I took a photo of Jake standing next to the Jeep, and it reminded me of an exact photo Dad took of me standing next to his Cadillac when I was about the same age.

As a set of waves started to roll in, I positioned myself to catch one to head back to the beach to check on Jenn & Jake. I found my wave, started paddling furiously, as the wave took control of my board, I stood up and rode the wave all the way back to the shore.

# THE TRIAL

....................

It was the beginning of fall 2009, I landed in Detroit and carpooled with my family to the courthouse in downtown Detroit. I was nervous as I was going to be in the same room with someone who was involved in the brutal murder of Dad. We made our way through security and were waiting outside the courtroom for the trial to begin. It was extremely uncomfortable that we were in the same waiting area as the family of Doyle Palmer, who was involved in the crime. There was a clear difference in class between our families. The courtroom doors opened, and everyone filtered into the open bench seats. They escorted in Doyle Palmer shackled in an orange jump suit. Doyle was a small guy; about 5'4" and earned the nickname "Shorty." Both sides of the legal teams took their seats on opposite sides of the courtroom. It was a long session with both sides presenting the details of their case.

Doyle had changed his story multiple times leading up to the trial, but his latest story was that he went home with Dad the night of the crime to sell him some cocaine and were both surprised by a group of young teenagers already in the house. According to Doyle's story, he and Dad were held at gunpoint upon entering the house. They were escorted up to Jack's room to be shown what the teenagers had done to Jack and threatened Dad & Doyle that they would end up the same way if they didn't cooperate. According to Doyle's story, the teenagers were there for the safe in the garage, which they wanted Dad to open, but on the way back down to the garage, a scuffle broke out, and Doyle was able to escape the house, running off to safety and unaware of what happened after.

The prosecution presented evidence of a latex glove found at the house that had Doyle's blood on the inside and Dad's & Jack's blood on the outside of the glove. They had also found a knife at the house that had blood from Doyle, Dad, and Jack. In presenting a video from the interrogation of Doyle a few days after the crime, the prosecution pointed out that he had a visible cut on his hand that had matched a cut in the glove. In the video, Doyle also had a large bruise on his forearm and a black eye. At the time of the interrogation video, the police released Doyle Palmer from custody, writing off his cuts and bruises as Doyle had mentioned he was in a recent fight not related to the crime at Dad's house. The prosecution presented their case: they believed Doyle was at the house with a plan to take the safe from the garage, but then Dad & Jack unexpectedly returned to the house earlier than expected.

The prosecution believed those involved were shocked to find Jack at the house once inside. The prosecution believed the suspect(s) entered either through the downstairs sliding door on the back porch or through Jack's upstairs balcony sliding door. Jack was brutally stabbed seven times and shot nine times in his bed. They believed Dad then pulled up to the house, entered through the side door next to the garage door, and he was immediately attacked and stabbed to death in the garage. I kept imagining a glimpse of Dad's expression as he came through the door and was surprised by the intruders.

Those involved doused the garage with gasoline and placed accelerants in the upstairs bedrooms to spread the fire throughout the whole house in attempt to burn the house down, destroying any evidence. The accelerants in the upstairs bedrooms had distinguished themselves leaving the fire concentrated in the garage. The prosecution believed the safe was taken from the garage before the fire was started at the house, then those involved drove Dad's work van a few blocks away, emptying the contents before setting it on fire. The fire department was able to put out the fire in the garage before it spread to the rest of the house. Dad's charred body was found the next day underneath a pile of debris from the storage loft and roof, which had collapsed as part of the fire in the garage. When describing the condition of how Dad

& Jack were found, they gave the courtroom a heads-up that they were going to show graphic images of their remains. I put my head down to avoid seeing any of the images while the prosecution presented images of Jack's wounds and pictures of Dad's charred body.

During a break, I heard a rumor that Doyle had planned to sneak a shank into the courtroom with the intent to stab his own legal team but was stopped in the process. It sounded like he wasn't happy with how his legal team was handling the case. During the trial, they had also brought in a few suspects for questioning, one of whom was Jeff Peterson. Even though it seemed obvious this wasn't a one-man job, the police department didn't have enough concrete evidence to convict anyone outside of Doyle Palmer for these crimes. Dad & Jack's case wasn't a big priority for the police department given some of the other high profile cases going on at the time. Doyle Palmer was given back-to-back life sentences without chance for parole, and the case was considered closed. Doyle knows exactly what happened that night at Dad's house and there is always the chance he will decide to reveal the details before he passes away in prison.

While heading to the Detroit airport to head home, I received an instant message on Facebook from Dad's ex-girlfriend Misti. She was now living in Huntington Beach, which is right next to Newport Beach. The timing of it all was so crazy; it almost felt like Dad was trying to reconnect us after all these years. Before my flight, we exchanged a few messages. I mentioned everything going on, and we set up some time to get together when I was back in town. During my flight home from Detroit, I thought about my very last interactions with Dad.

# FINAL MOMENTS

. . . . . . . . . . . . . . . . . .

During September of 2007, Jake was two months old, and Dad made plans to fly out to Orange County to visit his newborn grandson. I reserved him a room at the Westin next to South Coast Plaza, which was right down the street from our apartment. Dad arrived late afternoon and took a taxi to the hotel since I needed to finish up some things at the office. I arrived at Dad's hotel room and knocked on the door. I was excited for him to see me dressed for business in a sport coat and dress slacks. Dad opened the door, and happy to see him, I gave a big hug. We went into Dad's room as he wasn't quite ready to head over to our apartment. While he was changing, I told him I had something to show him. I took off my sport coat and unbuttoned my dress shirt to showed him my tattoo of Jake's name on my left breast. Dad kind of chuckled and asked if he should get one while in town that said, "Brett." We laughed as Dad finished getting ready. I asked if he was ready to go meet his grandson, and he nodded his head with a proud smile.

It was a very short drive to the apartment, and I told him how excited I was for him to meet Jake. We arrived at our apartment, and Jennifer opened the door with Jake in her arms. Dad was mesmerized at seeing his new grandson for the first time. Jennifer invited him to take a seat on the couch. Jenn handed Jake to Dad, and he placed him between his legs, facing him. I sat next to them, asking Dad, "Isn't he a good-looking boy?"

Dad proudly replied, "Are you kidding? He's the most beautiful thing I have ever seen."

Dad was so happy in the moment, checking out his newborn grandson. We spent all afternoon hanging out with Jake while Jenn and I told Dad about our life as new parents and being back down in Orange County. Since Jake

was still such a baby, we ordered food in for dinner that night before taking
Dad back to the hotel.

The next morning, Dad and I went golfing with a young real estate developer and his Dad. The developer was working with my friend Adam in the
build out of a new housing community in Costa Mesa called Canoe Pond
and we were considering one of the houses. The developer was still selling me
hard on buying one of the houses, trying to convince me it would be a great
investment for my family and I was getting in at a great time. When I mentioned to him my dad was in town, he invited us out for a round of golf with
him and his dad. I wasn't much of a golfer but knew how much Dad liked to
golf, so I figured he would love to play one of the local courses while in town.

The dynamic of our two father and son relationships was very different.
The developer and his father had what seemed to be a very stern relationship
while Dad and I were more like best buddies. During the course of the game,
the developer talked about the area of Newport and how great of an investment
the Canoe Pond neighborhood would be. We finished our game at Oak Creek
in Irvine with lunch at the country club and then went our separate ways.

Afterward, I drove Dad over to Canoe Pond, and we parked in front
of the house that we were close to pulling the trigger on a purchase. As we
sat out front in the car, I asked him what he thought about the little gray
house. I told him East Costa Mesa was where we wanted to live. I told him
the house was small, but the area was really expensive, so we couldn't afford
much more. Dad told me he thought it was a great house and loved the area.
He told me that he really wanted to be able to help with the down payment,
but cash was tight for him at the moment. He said if I could qualify on my
own, he would make up for it shortly with some cash to put toward the
house. I asked Dad again where that condo was where we spent the summer
with Misti that summer in the mid '80s, but he still wasn't sure of the exact
location as it had been so long. I told Dad that I couldn't believe I now had
a son and was settling down all these years in the same area. I reminded Dad
of my fond memory of him buying me my first skateboard on the boardwalk
in Newport Beach and told him that surf shop was still there. Dad's support

for me buying the house was the final straw for me to put things in motion to purchase the house.

We spent that afternoon back at our apartment, spending time with Jake. The next morning, I drove Dad to the Orange County airport to catch his flight back to Detroit. Parked outside the terminal, I got out of the car to give him a hug and told him how much I loved him. Dad told me he loved me and was so proud of me. I watched Dad walk through the sliding glass doors at the front of the airport, and that would be the last time I saw him in person.

In late January 2008, I called Dad on a Saturday afternoon while driving through the mountains heading back from snowboarding in Big Bear. During the winter months, I loved taking day trips snowboarding, waking up early to drive two hours up into the mountains, snowboard all day, and then drive home. I called Dad on my way to tell him about my day as snowboarding always reminded me of him. I caught Dad while he was out servicing his customers, and we talked for a while about my day out on the mountain. Dad told me that he had always wanted to ski Big Bear and that he would make a trip back out there soon to spend a weekend with me skiing. I said it was probably not that much different from Boyne Mountain in Michigan where he normally skied in the winter. Dad laughed and told me I was crazy as Big Bear was so much bigger. Dad asked for the peak elevation of Big Bear. I said about seven thousand feet, and Dad said, "Well, Boyne is about seven hundred feet." We laughed at the comparison as I couldn't remember how big Boyne was; I hadn't been in years, so it seemed similar in my mind.

Dad asked about Jake, and I told him I couldn't wait until Jake could start skiing with me. I told him we were starting to feel settled in at our new house in Canoe Pond after spending our first holiday season together as a family in the house. Dad told me he had to run as he was at one of his customers' bars, so we wrapped up our call with me telling him I loved him. Dad told me he loved me too, and that was the last discussion I ever had with him.

# ALTERNATE ENDING

....................

I landed in Orange County from my flight home from the trial. I was still pretty shaken up from the trial, which had ripped back open the wounds that had started to heal over the past year and a half leading up to it. As I walked through the airport, I continued to think about how there was more involved in the murders, but those threads were no longer being pursued by the police as the case was now considered closed. I walked out of the airport to find Jenn and Jake waiting at the curb to pick me up. I gave Jenn a kiss and turned around in my seat to say hi to Jake in his car seat. We headed back to the house as I told Jenn about the trial. I walked into our house, looking at the black marble urn and still thinking about everything presented as part of the trial. That night, I settled into bed, and as I fell into a deep sleep, I had a dream I was in Dad's house the night of the murders.

I walked into the garage at the Canoe Pond house wearing a black hoodie, a plain black baseball cap, a black neck gaiter under my chin, jeans, and lace-up boots while carrying a shotgun in one hand and a duffel bag in the other. I placed them in the back of my topless green Jeep. I opened the garage and hit the road heading east. The wind was blowing through the cabin as I drove through Vegas, the mountains in Colorado, and across the Midwest toward Detroit. I pulled up to Dad's house at night and parked a few houses down on the street. I grabbed the shotgun out of the back of the Jeep and made my way to the door on the side of the house next to where the safe was located. I picked the lock, entering the garage, and closing the door behind me.

Standing in the garage and looking around, it was exactly how I remembered it the last time I was in town for Christmas with Dad almost ten years ago. I stood there for a moment, looking at the Cadillac with the moonlight reflecting off the white metallic paint, filtering in through the tall, skinny windows along the wall of the driver's side facing the street. I propped the shotgun up against the wall next to the door by the safe and walked to the driver's side door of the Cadillac. I opened the door and got behind the wheel for a few minutes, thinking about that night driving around with Dad & Jack the last time I was in town.

As I was sitting in the car, a few sets of headlights slowly pass by through the tall, skinny windows. I became nervous as I knew it was those who were responsible for what was to unfold at Dad's house. I got out of the Cadillac, put my hoodie up, and pulled up the neck gaiter over my mouth and nose so only my eyes were visible under the brim of my ball cap. I walked over and grab the shotgun propped up next to the door. I stood next to one of the garage windows out of sight, looking out and waiting for them to approach Dad's house. As they started to walk along the side of Dad's house, making their way to the backyard, I opened the door next to the safe to greet them with the barrel of the shotgun point-blank. Completely caught off-guard, the suspects froze in their tracks and scattered off.

In the dream, it wasn't clear how many were at the house. I stood in the doorway with the shotgun by my side as the sound of tires squealing was heard off in the distance. The view transcended up above the house and over to the other side of town with Dad walking out of the Chas Bar and getting into his van to head home. In my dream, I saw Dad making his way back to the house from above. Then headlights lit up the garage as Dad pulled into the driveway. I put my hoody down, pulled my neck gaiter back down, and propped the shotgun back up against the wall as I headed into the house from the garage just as Dad was coming through the side door.

I helped Dad open the door from the inside to greet him, and he wore the same expression I imagined him having when he was surprised by the intruders. His expression changed to a smile as he realized it was me hugging him in the door. Dad asked what I was doing back in Detroit. I told him that I just missed him and wanted to see him. Excited to see me, Dad invited me into the kitchen for a drink. We walked down the entry hallway toward the kitchen with my arm around him. As we entered the kitchen, Jack came downstairs, visibly woken from a deep sleep to see what all the excitement was about. I gave Jack a hug and told him I just wanted to surprise Dad.

Jack said, "Well, you guys catch up. It's good to see you," and headed back up to bed. Dad asked what I wanted to drink. I asked for a whiskey on the rocks. Dad poured himself a vodka and soda. We clinked our glasses over the island in the kitchen. The dream ended with Dad asking, "How's Jake?" as I woke up next to Jennifer in our Canoe Pond house.

ROCKET MAN PHOTOS

......................

94-95 VAIL & BEAVER CREEK® RESORT

# COLORADO
# STUDENT

## BRETT LANGLEY
P52100139
RESTRICTED: UNTIL 11/27;
12/26-12/31; 2/18-2/20